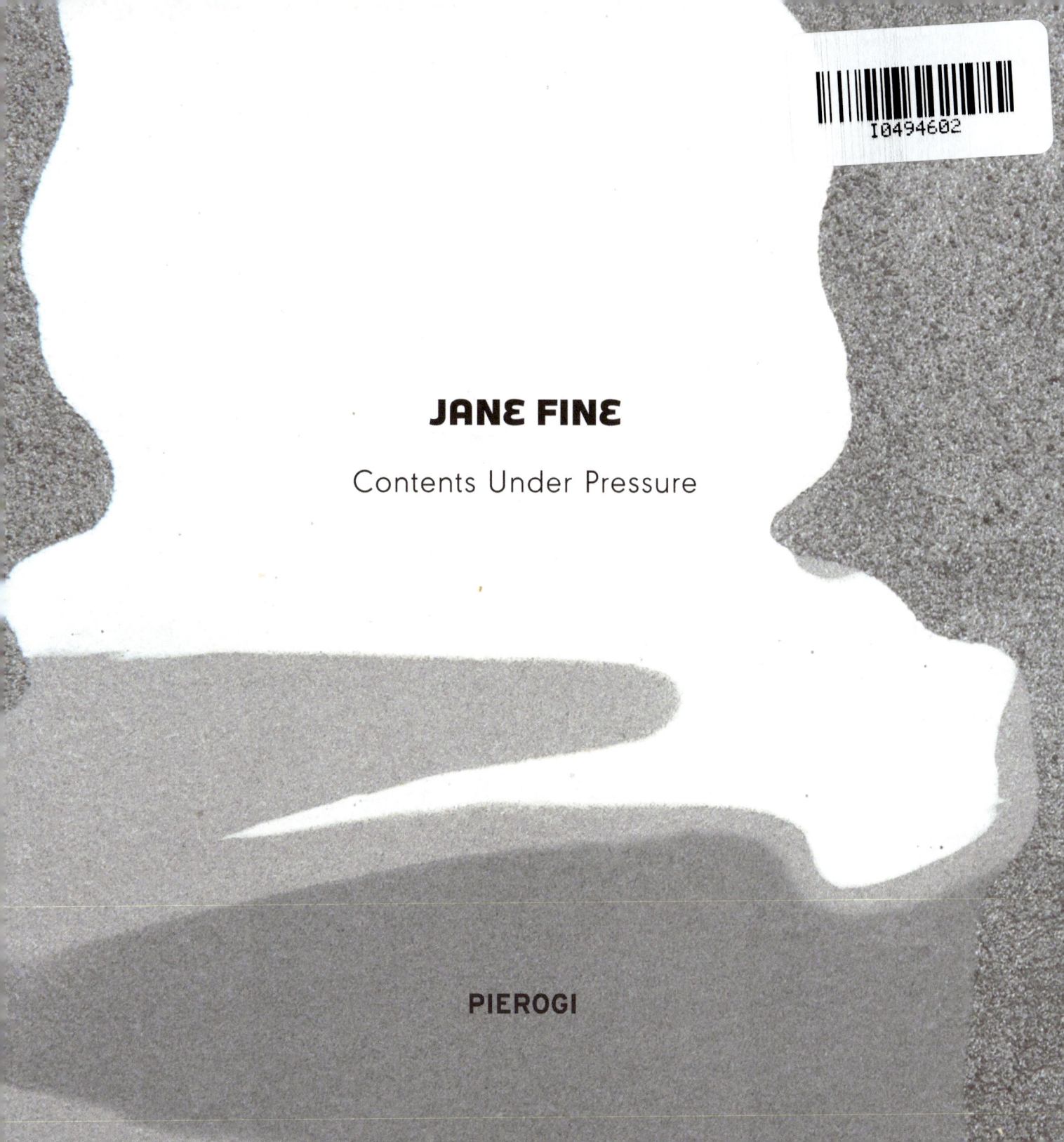

JANE FINE

Contents Under Pressure

PIEROGI

FOR JAMES AND ABRAHAM, WHO CONTINUALLY INSPIRE ME;
FOR JOE AND SUSAN, WHOSE HARD WORK AND GENEROUS SPIRIT ARE STUFF OF LEGEND;
AND FOR ALL MY FRIENDS AND FAMILY WHO NOURISH ME IN SO MANY WAYS.

THIS CATALOG WAS MADE POSSIBLE BY SUPPORT FROM THE OFFICE OF THE
DEAN OF THE FACULTY AT HAMILTON COLLEGE.

Published by Nauset Press
info@nausetpress.com
Design by Nauset Press

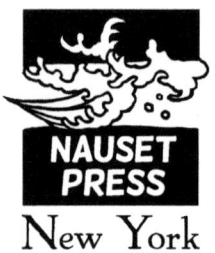

NAUSET
PRESS

New York

Text "Content Under Pressure", Copyright © 2016 Alan Gilbert
Interview "A Conversation", Copyright © 2016 Bruce Pearson and Jane Fine

Photography by: James Esber, Pierogi, and Polite Photographic Services

Front cover image: *Selfie*, 2014, acrylic on canvas, 32" x 50"
Back Cover: detail from *Selfie*, 2014
Title page: *Emergency Alert System*, (detail), 2015, acrylic on paper, see page 40 for complete installation

ISBN-13: 978-0-9907154-3-6

CONTENTS

CONTENTS UNDER PRESSURE

At the beginning of her interview (page 10) with the painter Bruce Pearson, Jane Fine states, "I'm an abstract artist at heart." This might seem odd, because what is initially so striking about Fine's work is both her unique sense of figuration and the constellation of objects she depicts: from flags, tanks, and collapsing brick walls to distorted faces and capital letters. And yet if you pause and look again, you'll see these images lodged within a cloud of frenetic color and line—bright, vibrant, and attacking geometry. This exploding energy in her work increased in urgency a decade ago as the global landscape transformed into unending war.

At the same time, Fine's paintings have an intimacy that makes their politics immediate and personal. As a viewer, you inevitably want to get close to her work in order to observe the different ways in which she applies paint; in the process, previously unseen images and figures are discovered embedded in the composition. And while much of her paintings' content may be sobering, there's a playfulness, even an exuberance, in the rendering—no dour political art here, however dark the humor. Instead of a program, a sense of uncertainty pervades Fine's work, one rooted in a mischievous freedom that endeavors to turn power on its head.

Take, for instance, all those flags—symbols of imperial conquest—in her recent paintings. They look rather dismal, and the territory they claim is rubble, as in *Duck and Cover Won't Save Us*, 2015 (page 8), or a toxic swamp in *Beetle Bailey Goose-Step*, 2015 (page 20). Fine reveals the authority these flags seek to represent as arbitrary and absurd—although no less deadly for that. Just ask the two maimed and bandaged figures in *The Veterans*, 2015 (page 14). Are they still fighting? Why does that flag look like a hatchet? Are they the product of ruin or have they produced it? Fine is less interested in answering these questions than in portraying the deep contradictions of contemporary life while also struggling to create meaning within them.

This sense of conflict—both serious and comical—gets extended to the domestic sphere with Fine's use of initials. As readers of her interview with Pearson will discover, the J., A., and J. that appear in her work are the first letters of the names of her husband, son, and, of course, Jane herself. In her paintings and drawings these initials are placed in various formal relations meant to mimic dynamics within the home—fun and banter, for sure, although as most of us know, families can also be stressful. The battlefield in Fine's work—ranging from cartoon to more direct representation—extends from the household to whatever country the United States decides to bomb next. Yet Fine's art holds out hope for something better from us and within us. The animated quality to its connections—via line, shape, and color—answers strife with enchantment. **—ALAN GILBERT**

Alan Gilbert is the author of two books of poetry, *The Treatment of Monuments* and *Late in the Antenna Fields*, as well as a collection of essays, articles, and reviews entitled *Another Future: Poetry and Art in a Postmodern Twilight*. He lives in New York.

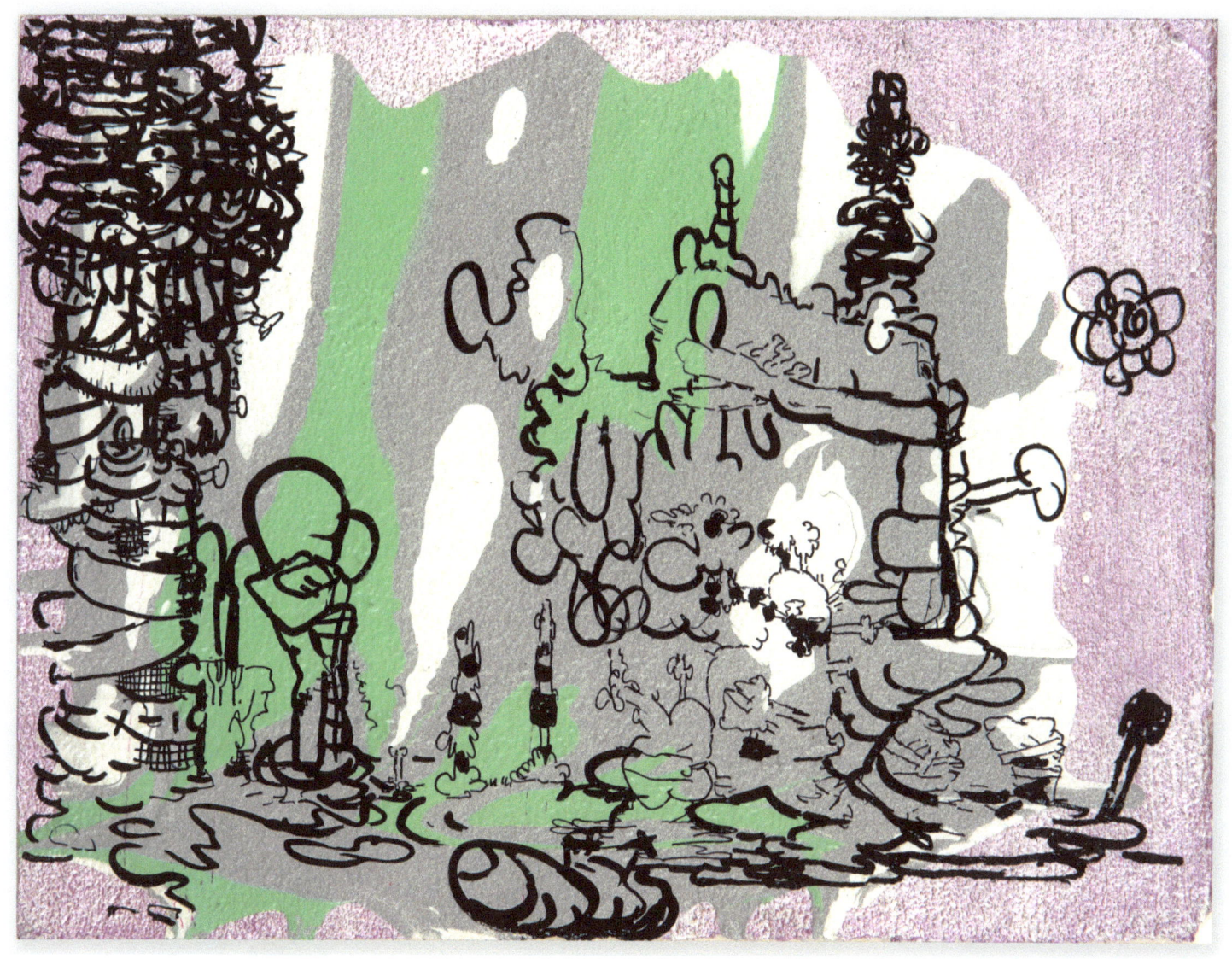

GAMEBOY

2015, acrylic and ink on paper, 9" x 12"

MY AMERICAN PAINTING

2015, acrylic on canvas, 74" x 55"

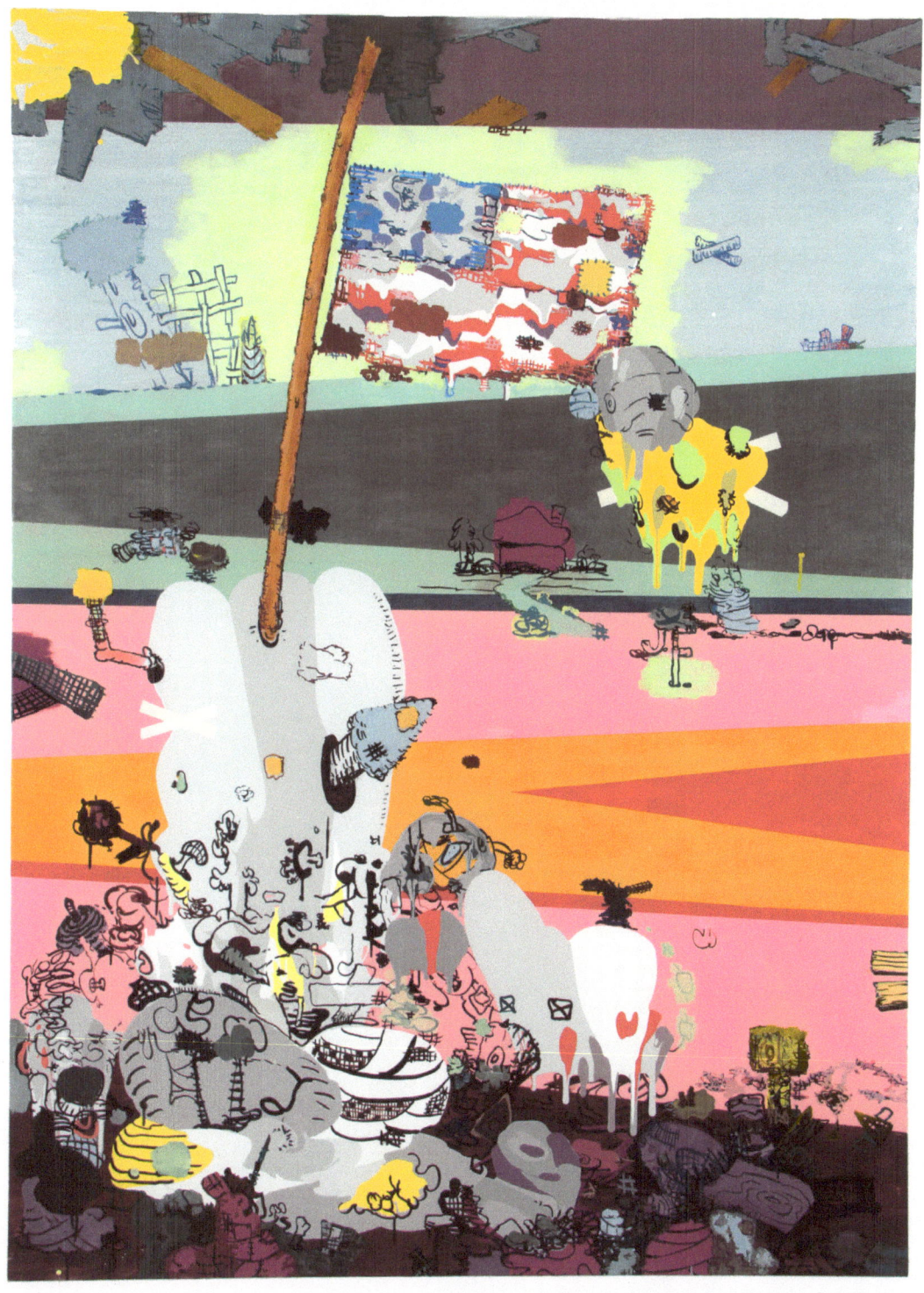

DUCK AND COVER WON'T SAVE US

2015, acrylic on canvas, 44" x 56"

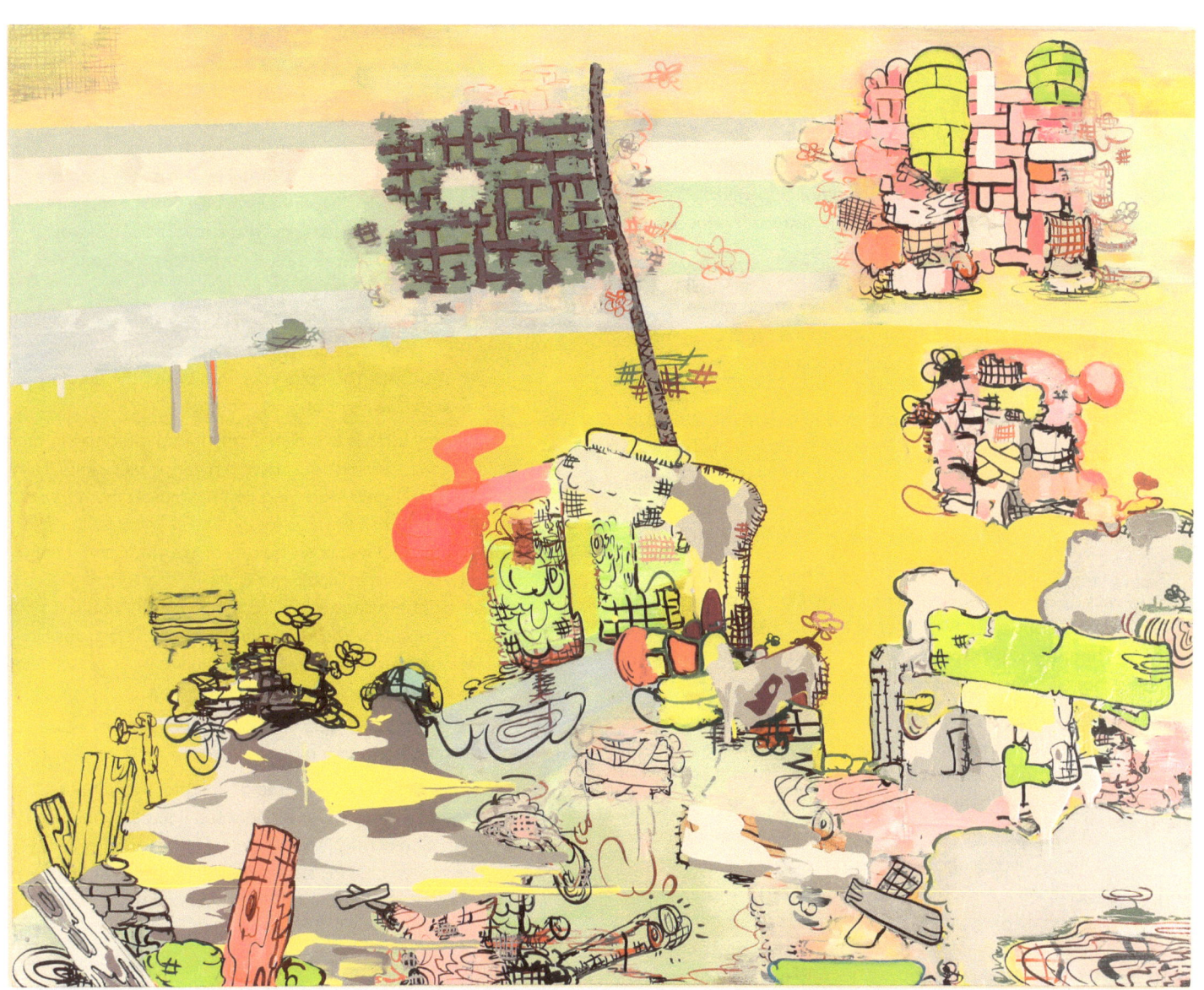

A CONVERSATION

Bruce Pearson sat down with Jane for a couple of hours in her Williamsburg studio. The two have been friends, neighbors, and admirers of each other's paintings for 25 years.

BRUCE PEARSON: There is an interplay of imagery and abstraction in your work. The cartoon-like imagery tends to be rustic (navy scenes, stone barricades, broken planks and bridges), but it is juxtaposed against a more fluid and evocative paint handling.

JANE FINE: Listen, I'm an abstract artist at heart. In high school, I wanted to be a theoretical mathematician. I studied math at Harvard. I was always interested in abstraction, I just ended up using a different set of tools.

I have this crazy desire to paint without looking at anything. I want the action to be between me and the canvas only. On certain days things flow so easily. On others, I feel I'm fooling myself, like I'm lacking the internal resources. I worry it's necessary to bring more figuration into the mix. Given the world we live in, I can't see working without some literal content. It feels imperative to have a connection to the world. I've come to think of my paintings as abstraction animated and contaminated by social content.

BP: The work's always moving in different directions, but has a striking consistency. Which ideas are most essential?

JF: The paintings are celebratory and joyous, but I'm filled with anxiety—about the climate, pollution, and war, not to mention about getting older, trying to make my work better. What interests me most is trying to deal with these extremes of emotion simultaneously.

BP: Apropos of anxiety, let's talk about your influences, your mother and father figures: Cecile Fine, your actual mother, and Philip Guston. Guston was in your earlier work but might not necessarily be there so much now.

JF: I learned about painting sitting on the basement steps in Queens, watching my mother paint. She was an object of fascination for me. She was very smart, often angry and unhappy, yet when she was painting she became transformed. She had a huge effect on me. I learned from her about my body in relation to the painting: how to move back and forth across the studio floor, to take risks with the material, and even to tilt my head in a certain way.

Although I met Guston briefly at Harvard, my true appreciation developed in art school, where everyone was in love with his paint's fleshy quality and the odd lumpiness of the depicted bodies. He taught me to paint with a sort of Jewish self-deprecating humor. I fell in love with how he combined pop culture and social consciousness. I think he's the first in the American vernacular who does this: he loved Krazy Kat as much he hated Kissinger.

BP: You've said that lately you're interested in George Grosz.

JF: My work's sweet, celebratory side always has come naturally, but the struggle has been how to best express the ugliness and anger. Recently I've looked to Grosz and Otto Dix. They both had horrid experiences fighting in World War I and continued to live in Germany during some extreme times. Grosz's satirical work has an edge that makes it feel remarkably contemporary. Do you know Dix's series of etchings, *The Art of War*? It really affected me—it almost makes Guston look silly.

BP: I know the series, yeah, though I find Guston's early and later works equally disturbing. You seem to be constantly reinventing yourself. You have your "Jane Fine" thing going on, but you're also always changing things up.

JF: One of my tricks is to switch up the formal parameters of my work, like daring myself to work with a very dark palette. I try to prevent repetition by screwing with my muscle memory. I'm teaching at Hamilton College for the year. My first studio there was tiny, just 10 x 11 feet and I quickly discovered I could only function by working in black and white.

To be fair (the college is funding this catalog!) I've been moved to a very nice studio. You know, this is one of the reasons I love artist residencies—when I'm away, my work always gets shaken up. I'm extremely affected by my environment.

BP: Over the last few years you've been doing these elegant, dark, dusk-like works that require close looking.

JF: Dusk became a powerful metaphor; that moment between day and night is like the border between figuration and abstraction. Sometimes I really miss the color. At a residency in Florida last year I couldn't stay away from fuchsia and turquoise. I suspect the next pieces will be predominantly dark, with small bursts of extreme color.

BP: You've been starting to use some letters, some language. How come?

JF: I wanted to make work about family dynamics. Ours is a triangle of three strong, creative personalities; two of us have names starting with "J" (Mom and Dad) and our son's name starts with an "A." I love the way that "A" is symmetrical and stable while "J" is off-balance. I turned the letters into snuggling, battling cartoon characters.

Meanwhile, we're in this ridiculous cultural moment where everyone craves self-representation, but of course artists have been doing that for thousands of years. Self-portraits are now selfies! I was looking for a new way to make a self-portrait, and I turned my initials into the subject; it's a signature as painting. The lettering is also inspired by the oddly tilted space of graffiti. I was thinking about how to depict confidence and I realized that the exaggerated pictorial space of graffiti accomplishes exactly that.

BP: This might be shop-talky, but you said you'd like to change your paintings' scale and do really big works.

JF: More than anything else, I want to make half a dozen huge paintings, as big as I can get in and out of the studio. I'm interested in visual contrast as a sign for emotional contrast. The bigger the painting is, the easier it is to accomplish that. I'd like to make a seven-foot brush stroke that radiates pure confident joy. Next to it I'll paint a congested, crusty tumor-like passage.

I love huge paintings, like Albert Bierstadt's or Frederic Edwin Church's, that make you feel you walk into another world. That crazy deep space seems so funny to me.

BP: I could really see you scaling up; it'd be awesome.

JF: I'm such a formalist nerd. We could sit here for hours and just bore everybody talking about matte and shine and thin and thick and crusty and...

BP Is there anything you'd like to discuss that we haven't talked about?

JF: Let me throw a question at *you*. I'm sure you get asked a lot about the community in Williamsburg; what do you think are some of the important aspects of the visual language that got passed back and forth between us?

BP: Interesting. People talk a lot about the Pierogi look, this intense graphic, energetic, compulsive, detailed look. How did the community influence and help form your own practice?

JF: The most significant thing for me was to have been immersed in this world. The level of intensity and seriousness was very important. We were so aware of being in it together. In terms of the visual language, it's partly what you call the Pierogi aesthetic, and also a shared love of pop culture and plasticky color.

BP: We were such outsiders for a long time. We were very much outside of what NYC was.

JF: Yeah, nobody was even showing paintings. It wasn't even

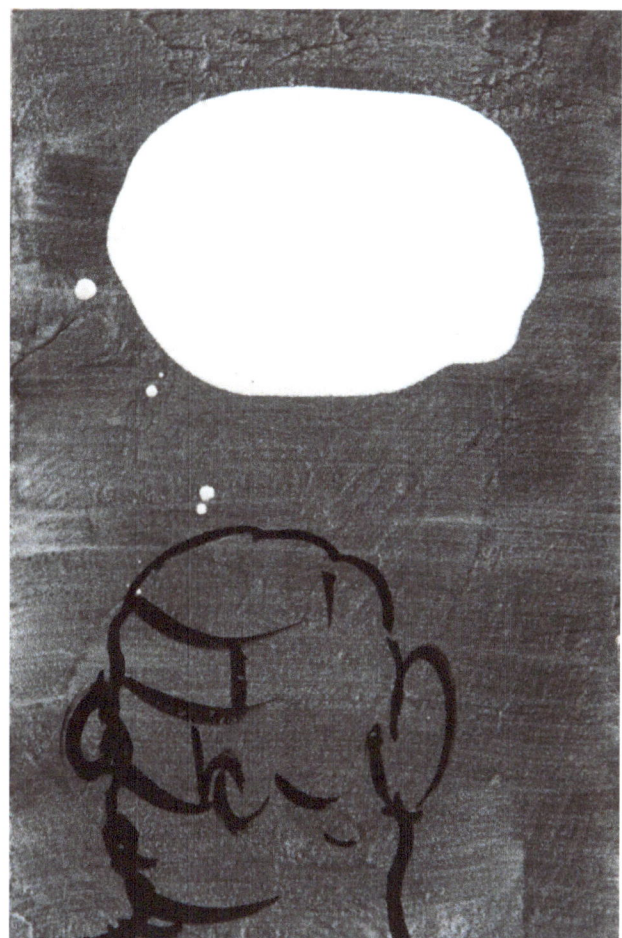

EMERGENCY ALERT SYSTEM, (ONE FROM SUITE OF 15 PAINTINGS) , 2015, ACRYLIC ON PAPER, 6" X 4"

about the *kind* of painting I was making, it was just the *idea* of painting that seemed so ridiculously outside.

BP: Doesn't that still seem true?

JF: I don't even know. Painting's dead, it's alive, it's back, it's selling, it's not selling, I can't even keep track anymore.

BP: Do you still feel like a "Brooklyn artist"?

JF: Look, it's all a part of my history. I'm a Brooklyn artist, a Jewish artist, a woman, a mother, a New York artist, a die-hard painter. But my community now is virtual: it's not about who I see on the street anymore, but about the twenty or thirty artists whose work I've known for decades who continue to inspire me.

Bruce Pearson is a New York based artist represented by Ronald Feldman Fine Arts.

MORNING COFFEE

2014, acrylic on paper, 21" x 29"

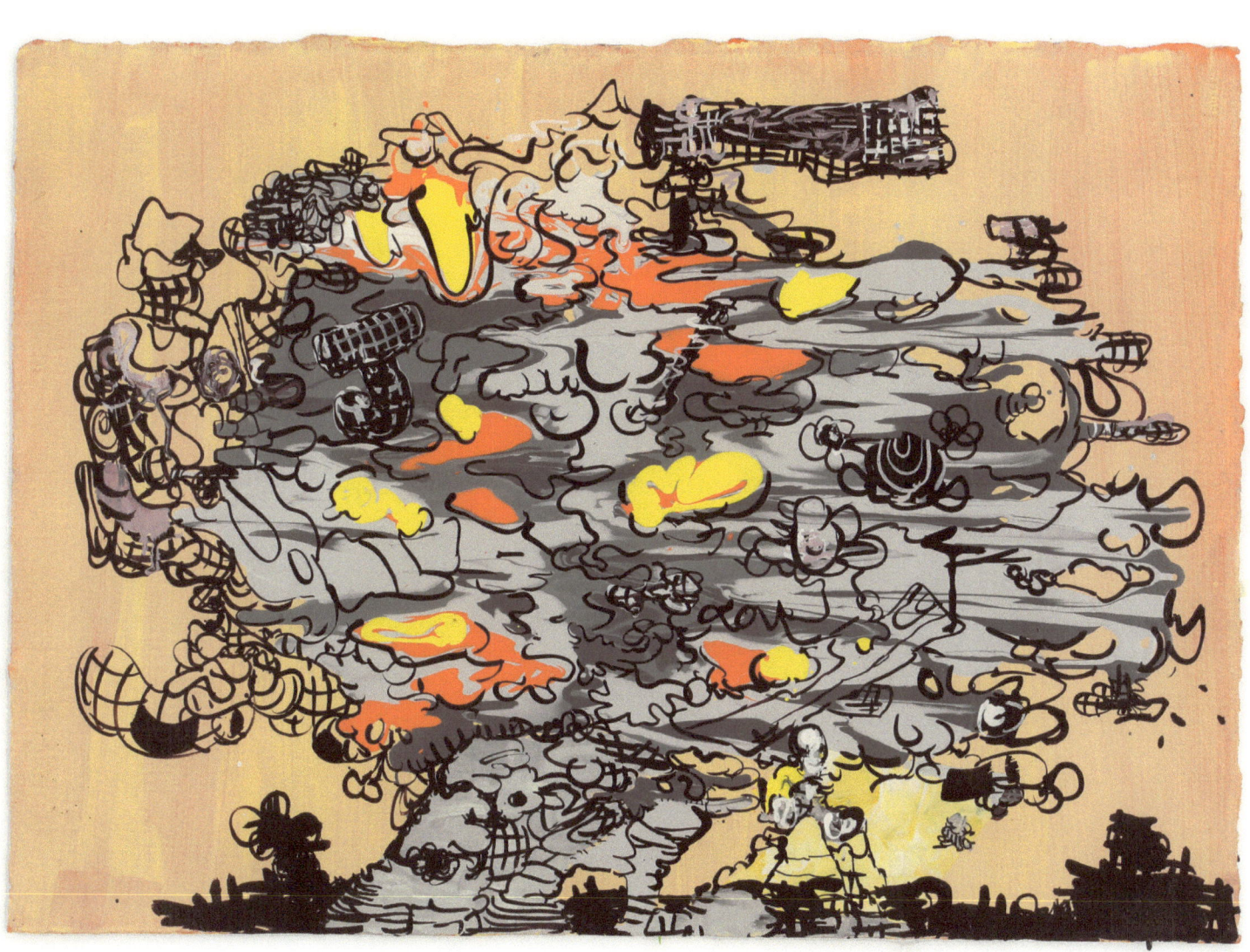

THE VETERANS

2012, acrylic on wood panel, 42" x 53"

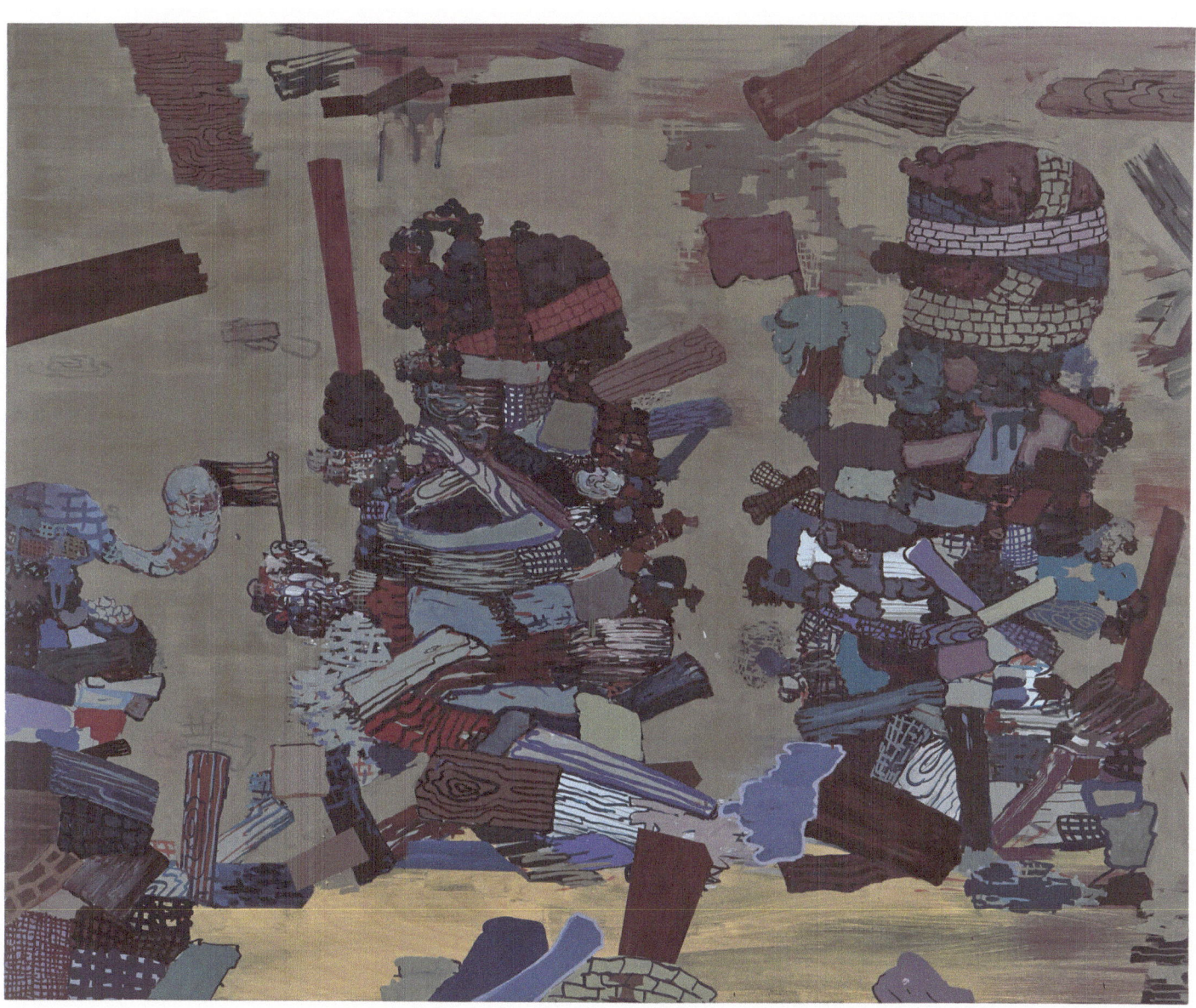

SELFIE

2014, acrylic on canvas, 32" x 50"

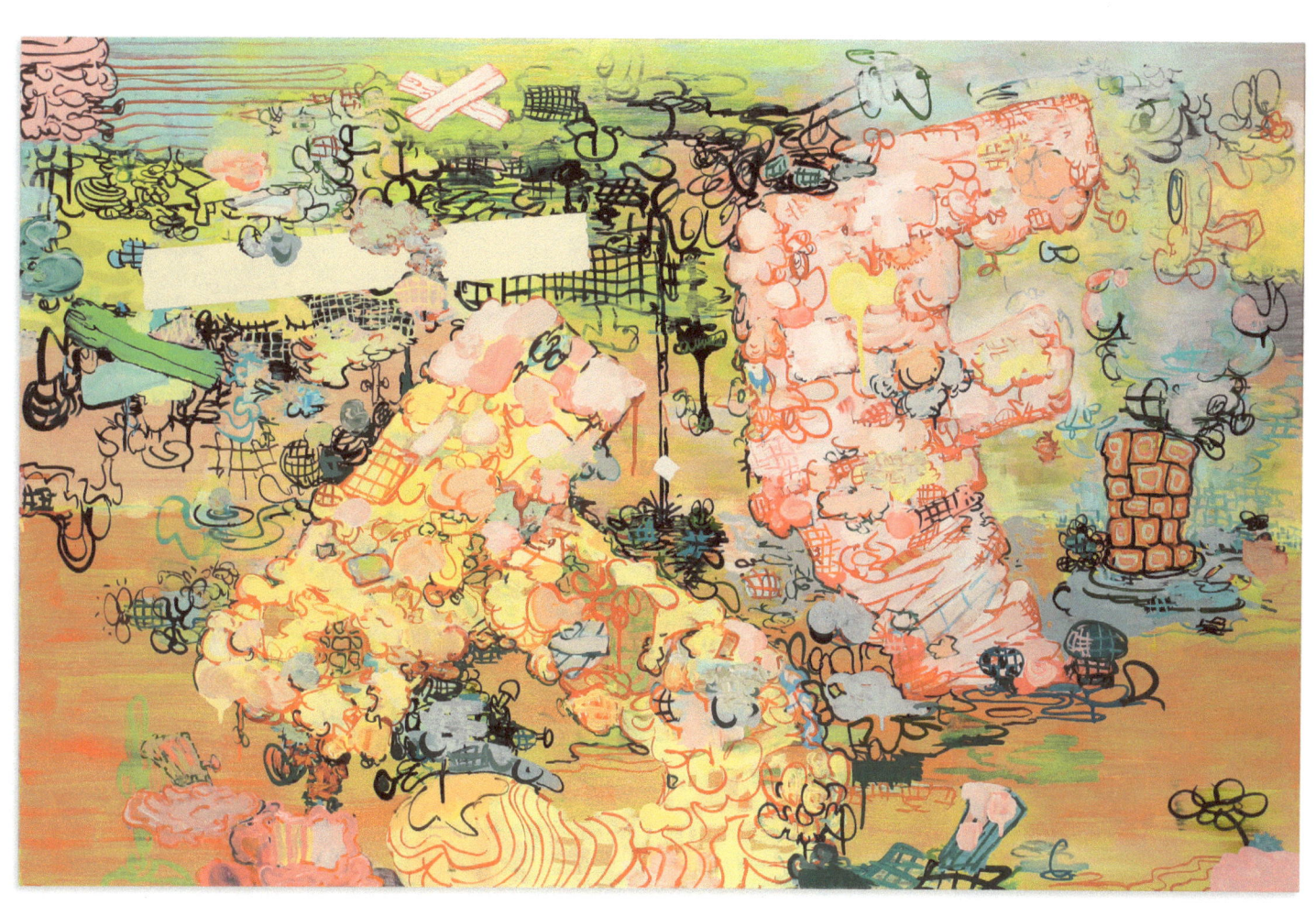

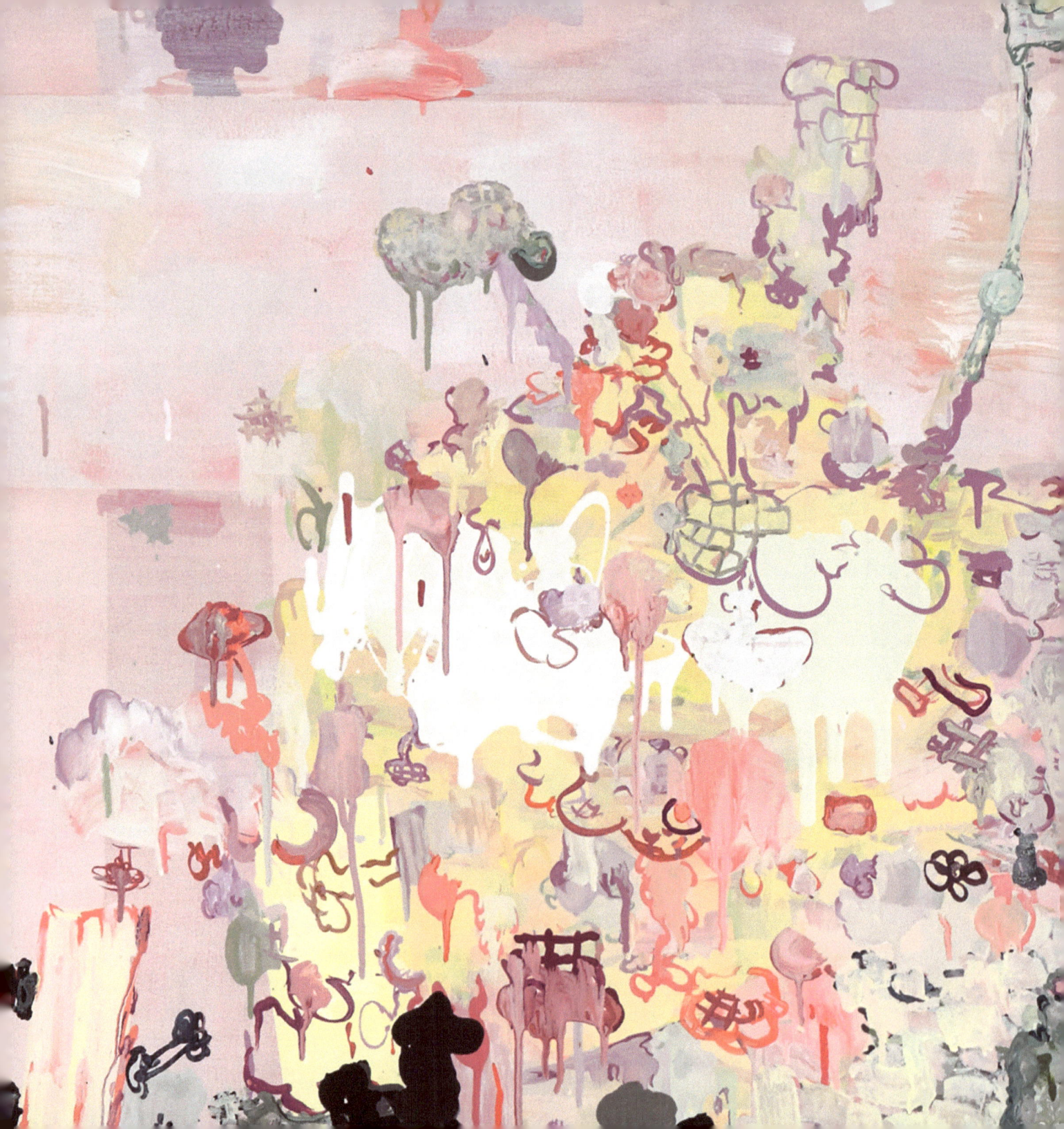

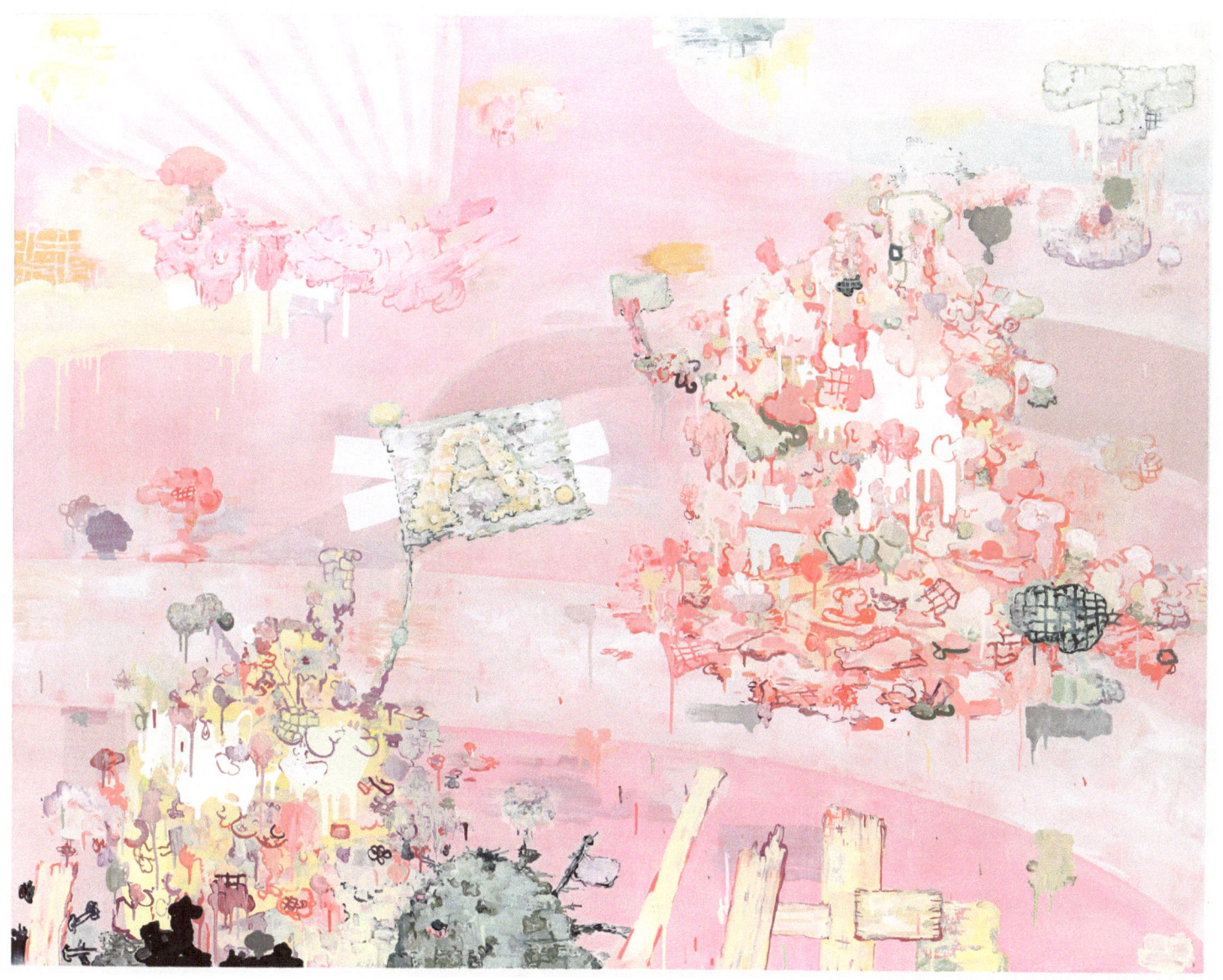

LADIES AND GENTLEMEN, PLEASE REMAIN CALM

2013, acrylic on canvas, 60" x 78"
Left: detail

BEETLE BAILEY GOOSE-STEP

2015, acrylic on paper, 30" x 22"

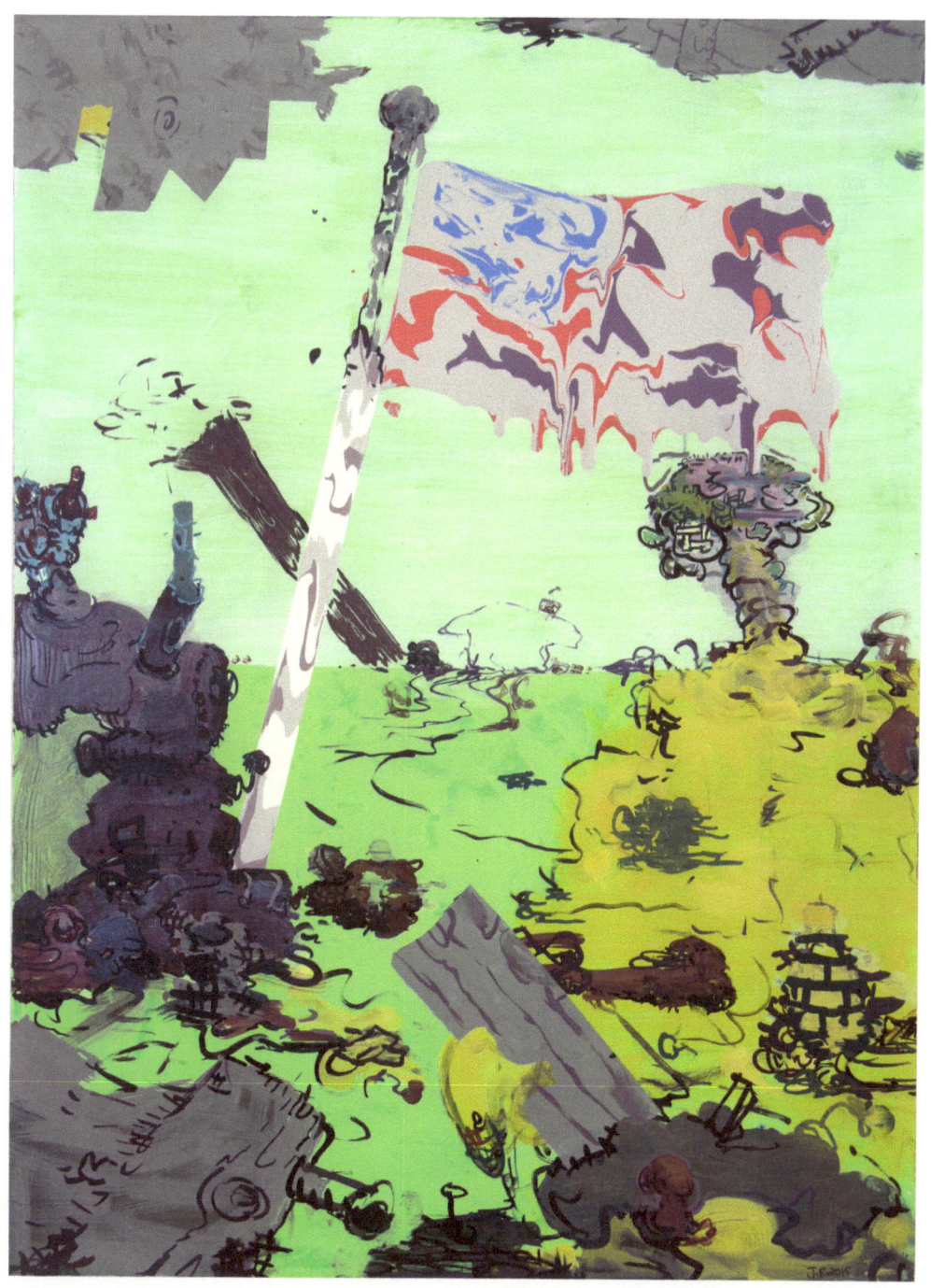

OMG, I MEAN POW

2015, acrylic on paper, 41½" x 29½"

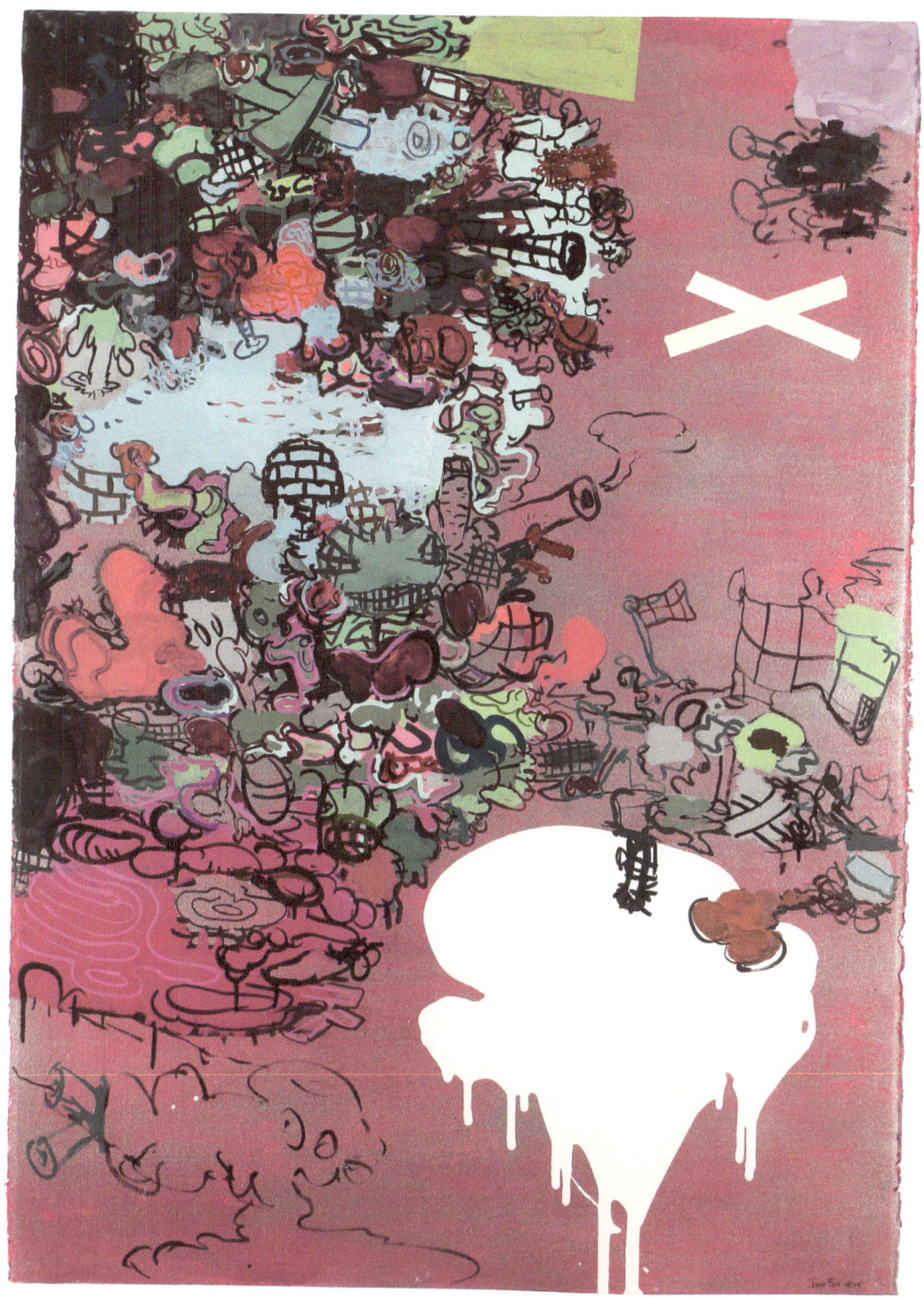

TAILSPIN À LA MODE

2015, acrylic and ink on paper, 30" x 22"

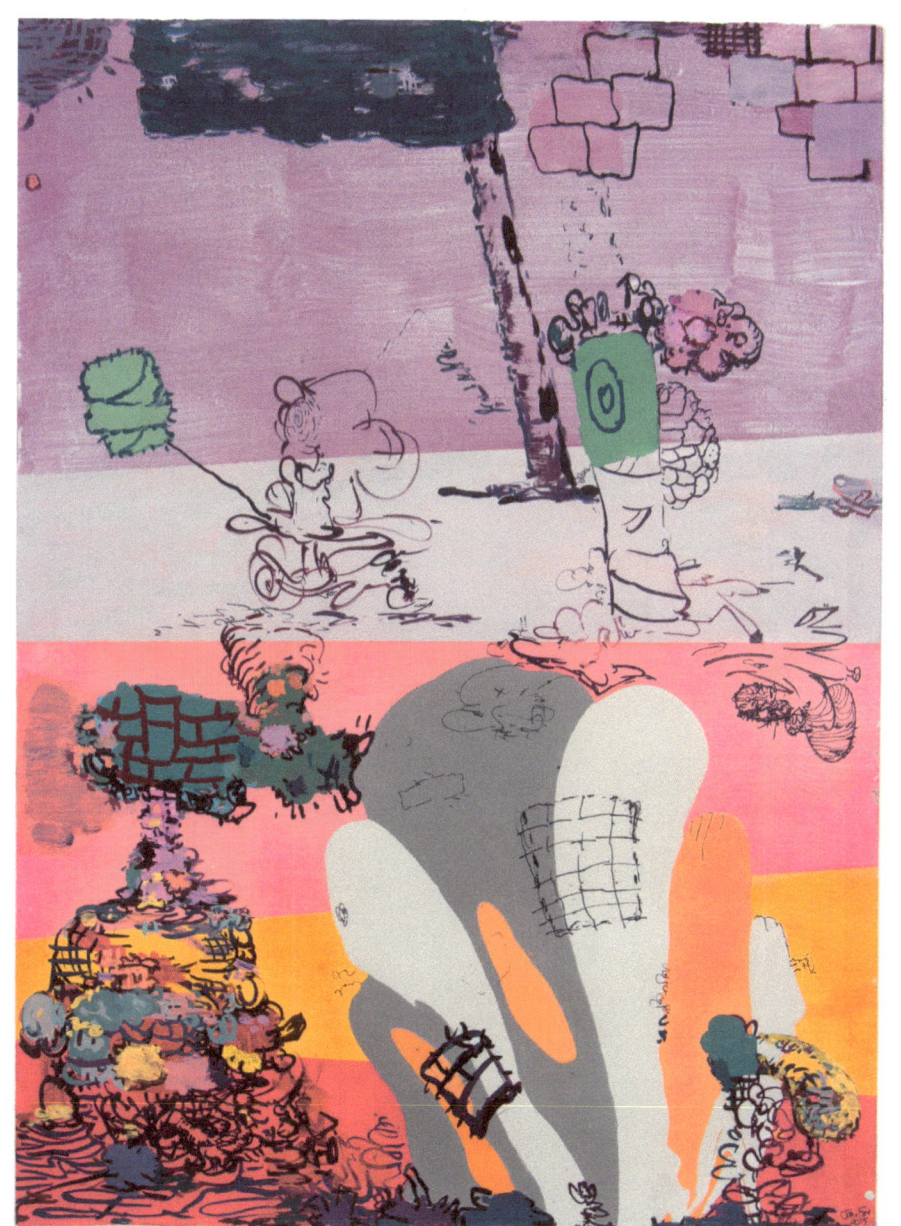

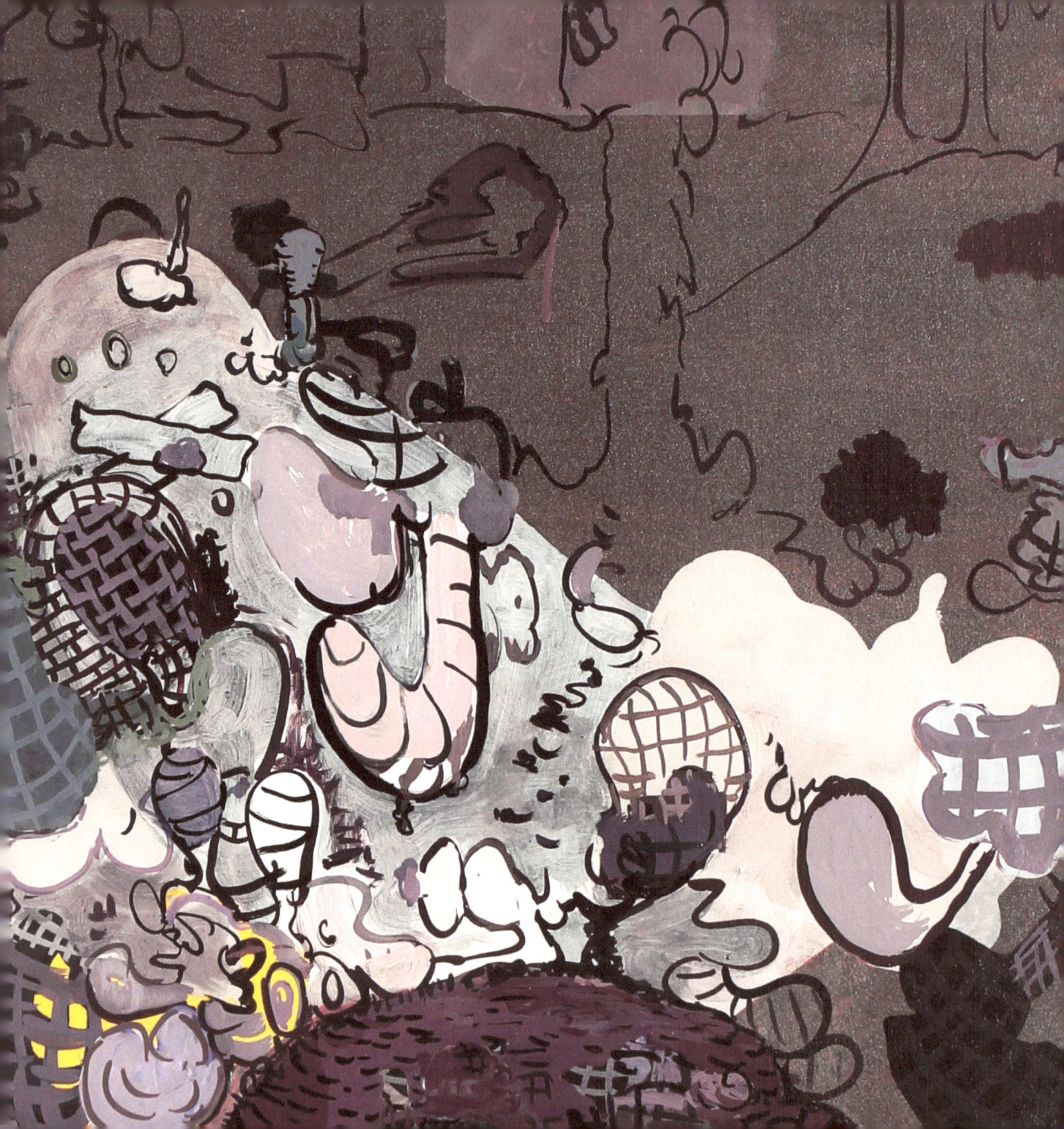

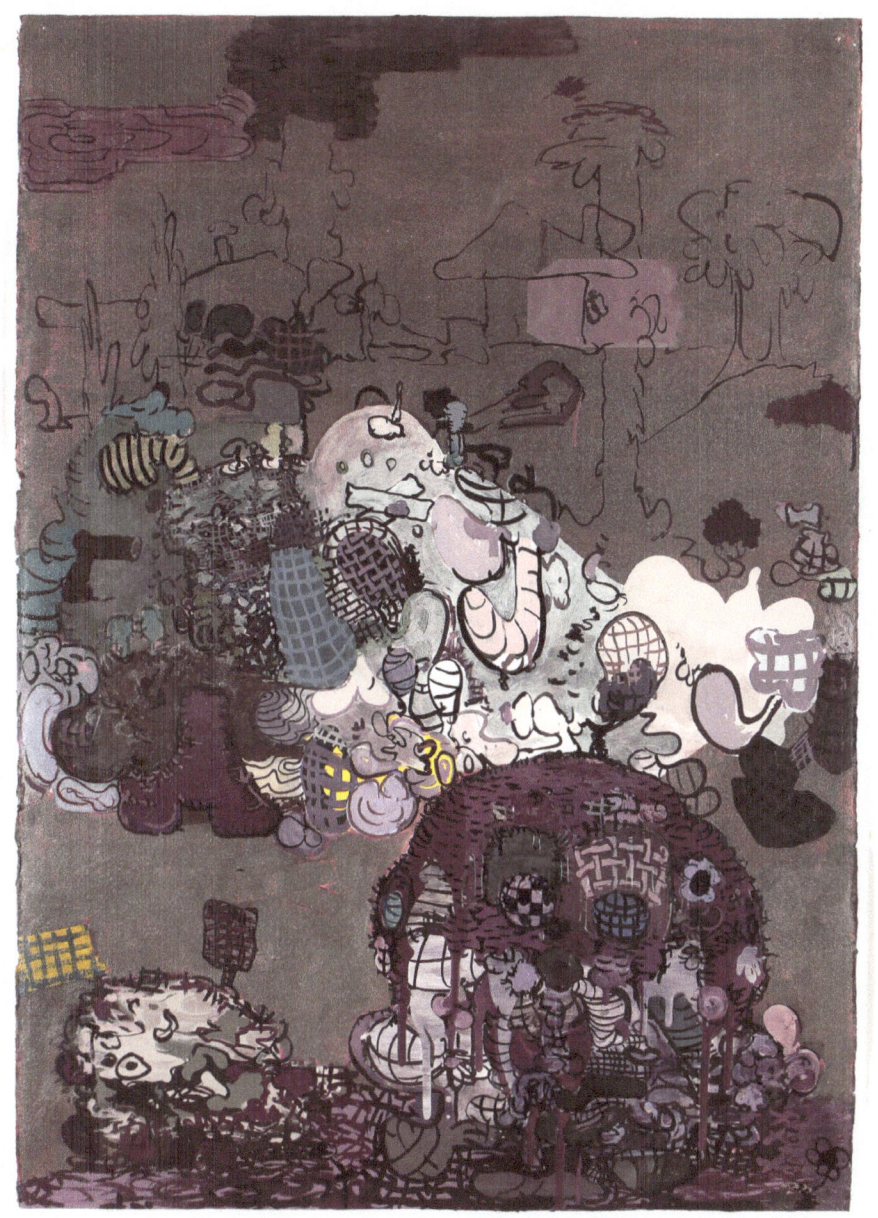

DUNG OF THE DEVIL

2015, acrylic on paper, 41½" x 29½"
Left: detail

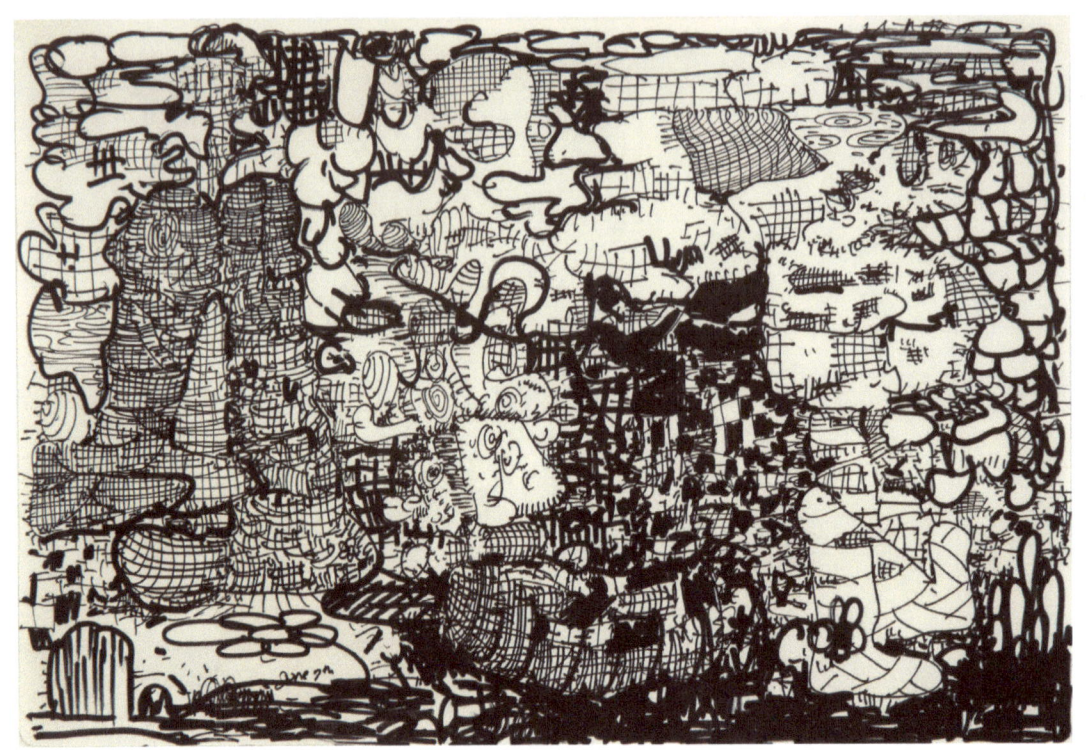

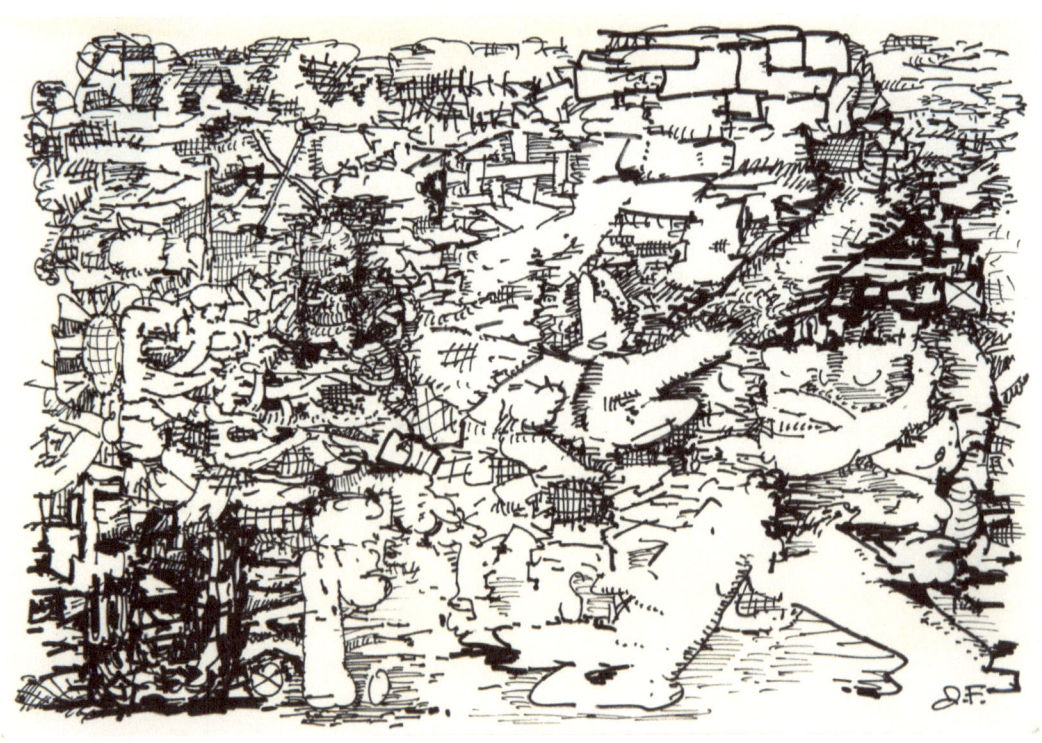

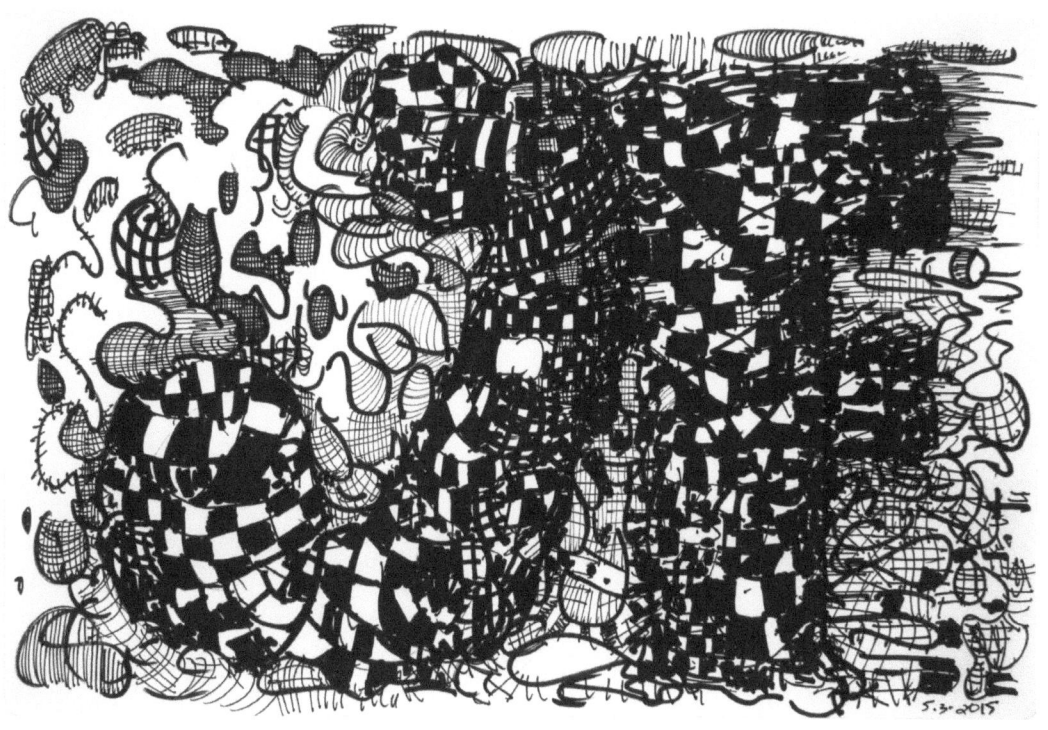

LETTERS ARE A BANDAID FOR SOMETHING WORSE

[SUITE OF 10 DRAWINGS]
2013-2015, ink on paper, 7¾" x 11¾" each

DO-OVER

2012, acrylic and ink on paper, 22" x 30"

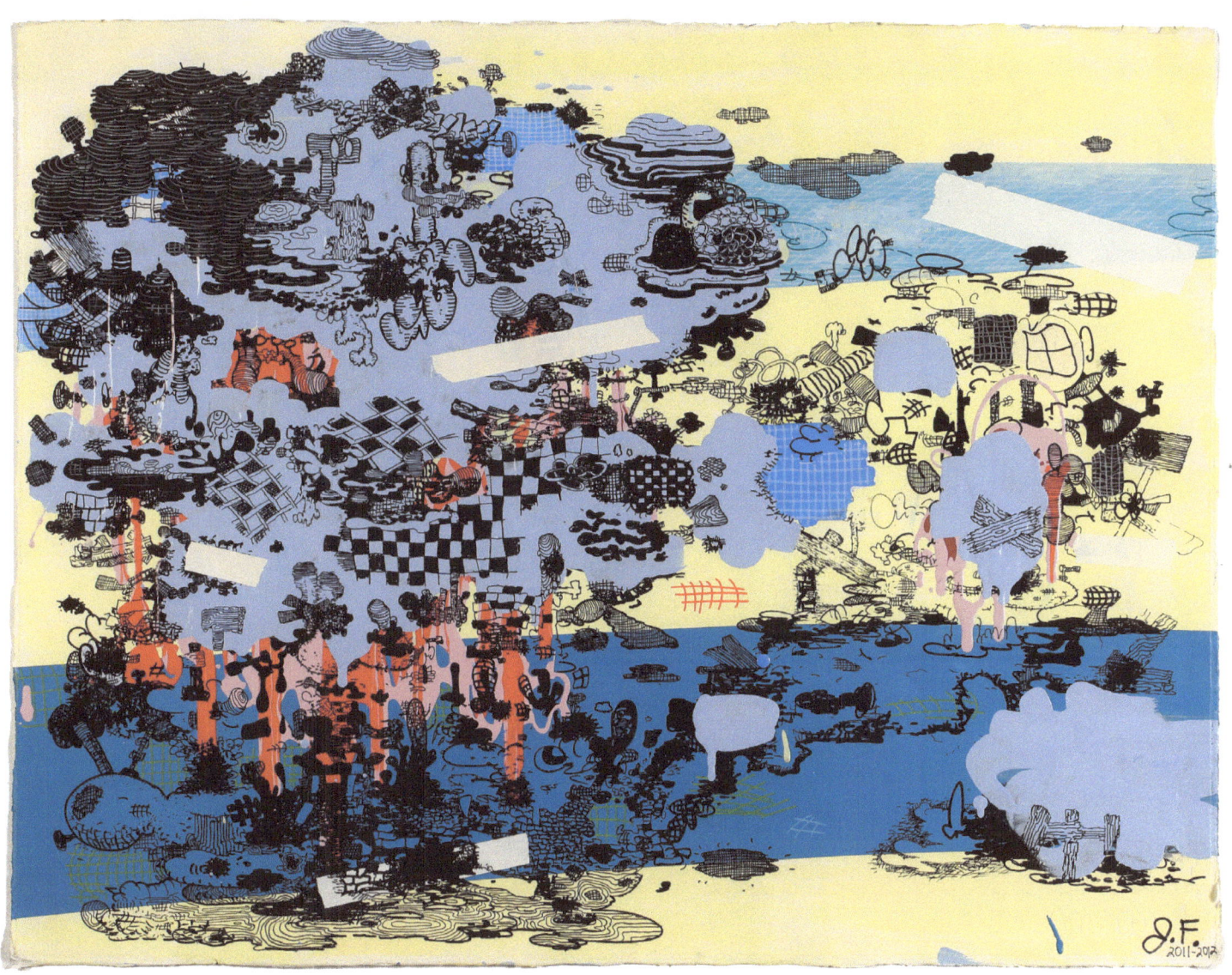

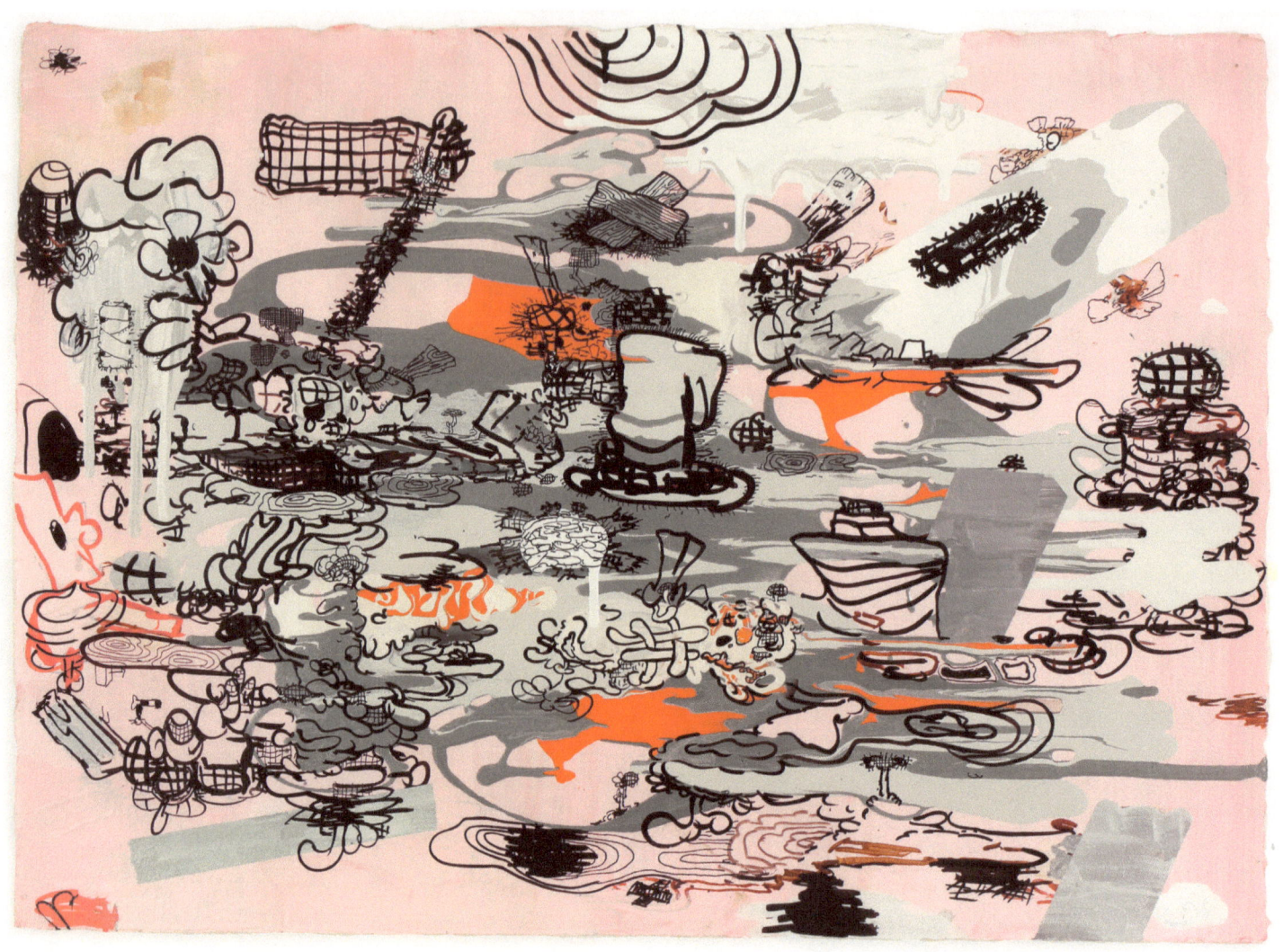

GIRL POWER

2014, acrylic and ink on paper, 20½" x 29"

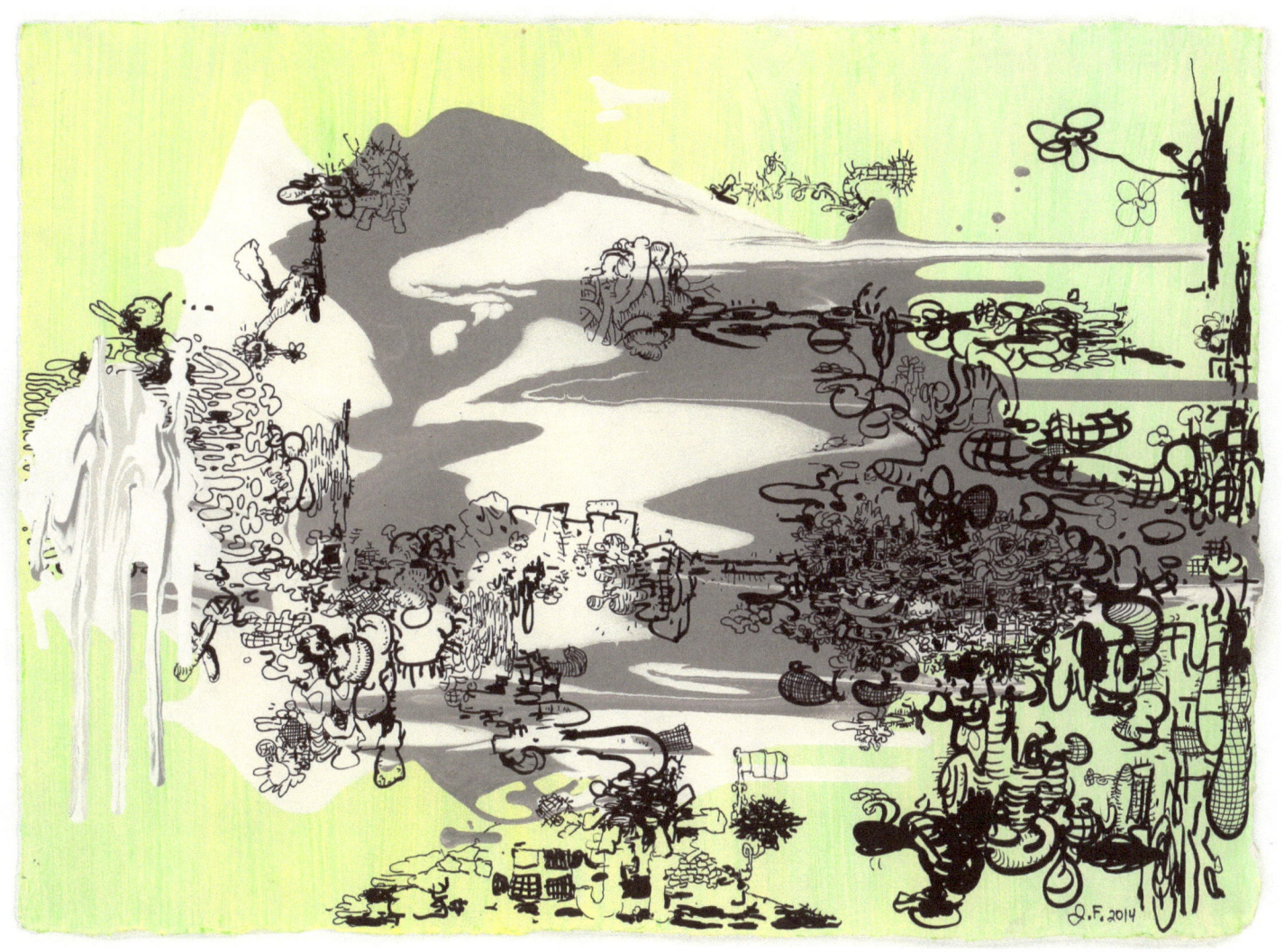

57TH VIEW OF MT. FUJI

2014, acrylic and ink on paper, 14½" x 20½"

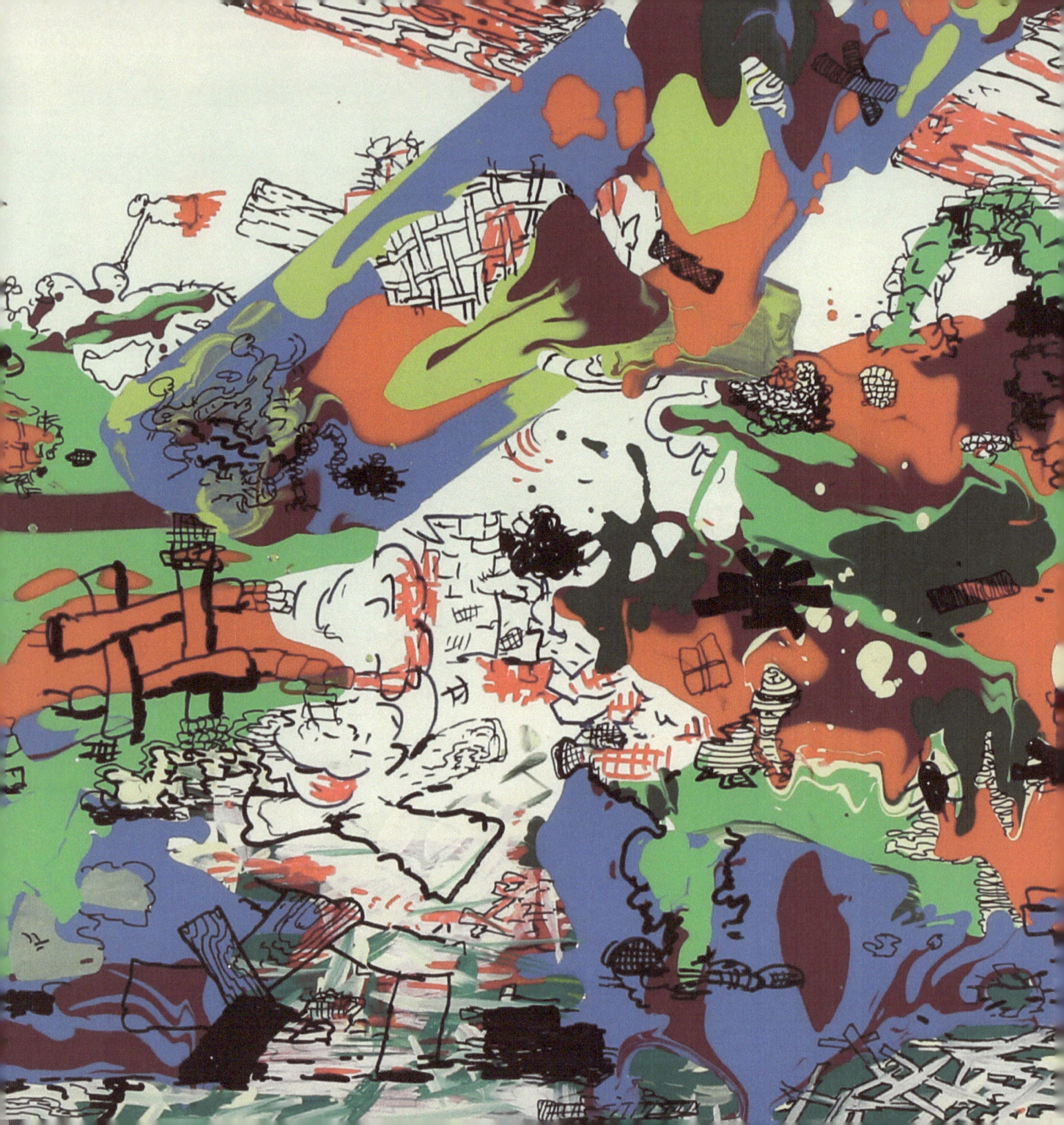

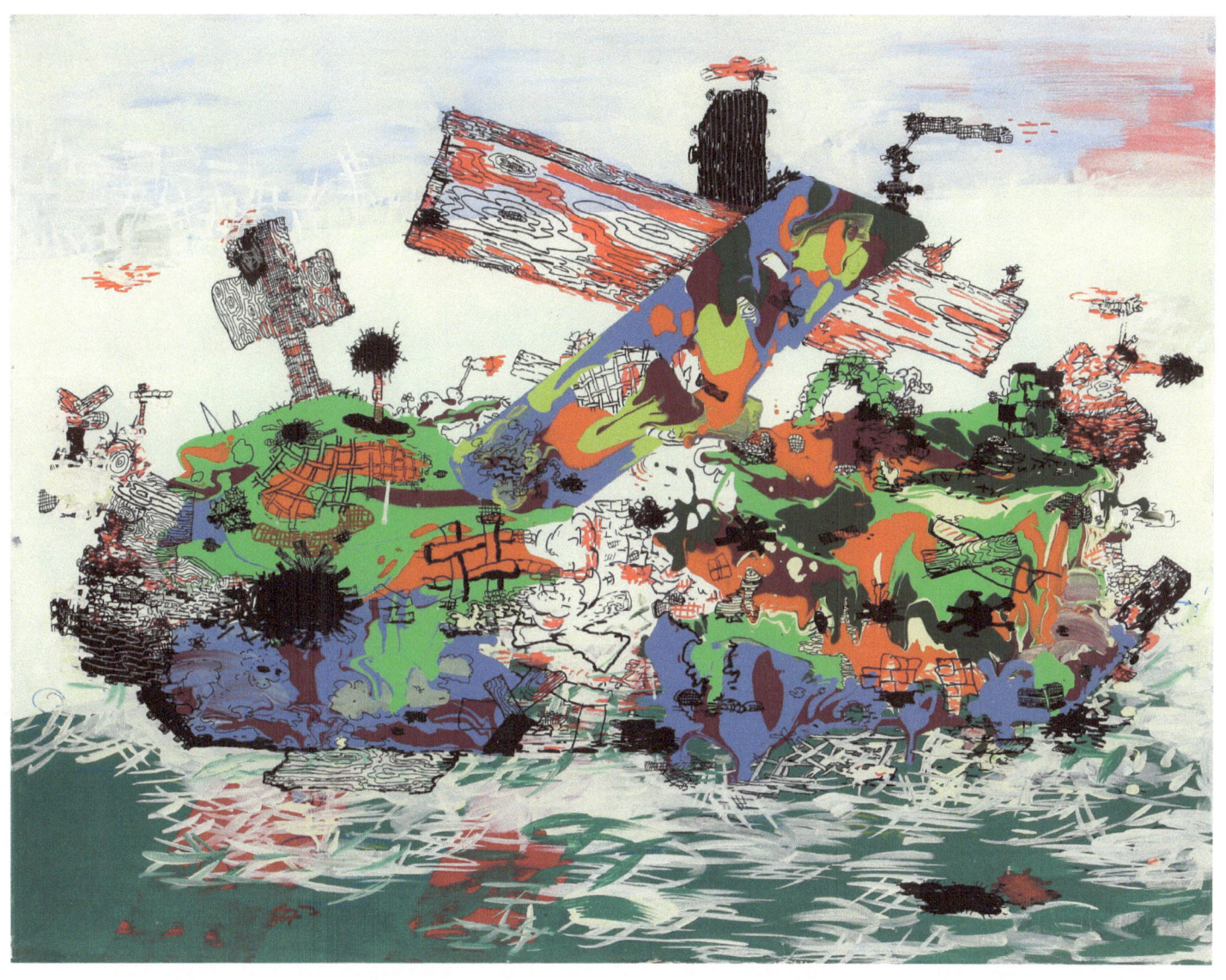

SINKING SHIP

2012, acrylic and ink on paper, 22" x 30"
Detail: Left

JANE FINE

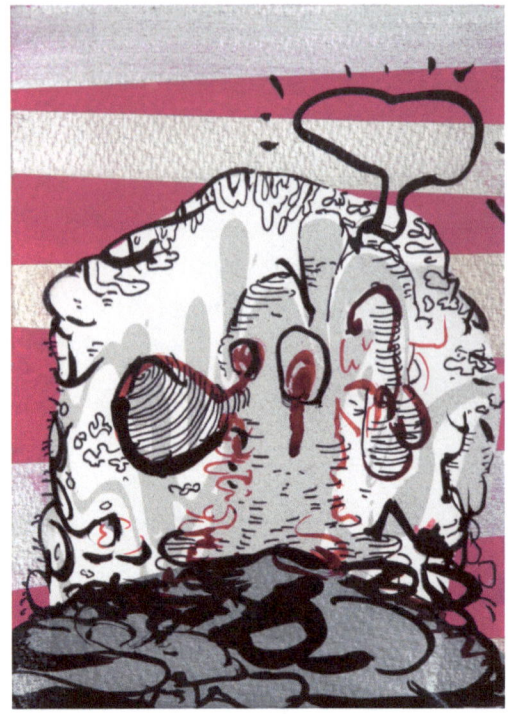

EDUCATION

1989	Skowhegan School of Painting and Sculpture, Skowhegan, Maine
1981-1983	M.A., School of the Museum of Fine Arts/Tufts University, Boston, Massachusetts
1975-1980	B.A., Harvard University, Cambridge, Massachusetts

AWARDS & FELLOWSHIPS

2016, 2015	○ Hermitage Artist Retreat
2013	○ Pollock-Krasner Foundation Grant
	○ Golden Foundation Residency, New Berlin, New York
2011	○ Yaddo, Saratoga Springs, New York
2010	○ Central City Artist Project, Artist-in-Residence, New Orleans, Louisiana.
2008	○ New York Foundation for the Arts, Fellowship in Painting
2001	○ Pollock-Krasner Foundation Grant
2001	○ Yaddo, Sally and Milton Avery Residency, Saratoga Springs, New York
1998	○ Cité Internationale des Artes, Residency, Paris, France
1998, 1996	○ Yaddo, Saratoga Springs, New York
1994	○ New York Foundation for the Arts, Visual Artists Fellowship
1992-1993	○ Fine Arts Work Center Fellowship, Provincetown, Massachusetts
1990	○ Millay Colony for the Arts, Austerlitz, New York
1989	○ National Endowment for the Arts, Visual Artists Fellowship

ONE-PERSON EXHIBITIONS

2016	○ "Contents Still Under Pressure," Englewood Art Center, Ringling College of Art and Design, Sarasota, Florida.
2015	○ "Contents Under Pressure", Pierogi, Brooklyn, New York
2014	○ "Ladies and Gentlemen, Please Remain Calm," Clifford Gallery, Colgate University, Hamilton, New York.
2013	○ "Fatty was an Angel," The Front, New Orleans, Louisiana
2012	○ "Formulas For Now," Pierogi, Brooklyn, New York.
2010	○ "Jolly Quagmire," Michael Rosenthal Gallery, San Francisco, California.
	○ "Where Boys with Guns Wear Bows in their Hair," (collaborative show with James Esber in conjunction with Prospect 1.5), The Wesley, New Orleans, Louisiana.
2009	○ "Glad All Over," Pierogi, Brooklyn, New York.
	○ "Border Patrol," AR/Contemporary, Milan, Italy

2008	○ "J. Fiber: World War Me", (collaborative drawing show with James Esber), Pierogi, Brooklyn, New York.
2007	○ "Skirmish", Pierogi/Leipzig, Leipzig, Germany.
	○ "Shock and Awe", Barbara Davis Gallery, Houston, Texas.
2006	○ "Friendly Fire", Bernard Toale Gallery, Boston, Massachusetts.
2004	○ "After Sugar Time," Pierogi, Brooklyn, New York. (catalog) Domo Gallery, Summit, New Jersey
2000	○ Pierogi, Brooklyn, New York.
1996	○ Casey Kaplan, New York, New York.
1995	○ Casey Kaplan, New York, New York.
1992	○ White Room, White Columns, New York, New York.

SELECTED GROUP EXHIBITIONS

2016	○ *Rage for Art (Once Again), Inaugural Exhibition*, Pierogi, New York, New York.
2015	○ *Pop-up Exhibition*, NYFA Curatorial/McKinsey & Company, New York.
	○ *Summer Faculty Exhibition*, Skidmore College, Saratoga Springs, New York
	○ *New Faculty Exhibition*, Fine Arts Work Center, Provincetown, MA

2014	○ *Pierogi XX*: 20th Anniversary Exhibition, Pierogi, Brooklyn, New York
2013	○ *Made in Paint*, The Sam & Adele Golden Gallery, New Berlin, New York
	○ *Unhinged*, Pierogi, Brooklyn, New York
	○ *Necessary Strangers*, AdventureLand, Chicago, Illinois.
2012	○ *image/clot*, Zolla Lieberman Gallery, Chicago, Illinois.
	○ *Cloud Nine*, The Front Room, Brooklyn, New York.
	○ *Drawing the Mind*, Osilas Gallery, Concordia College, Bronxville, New York.
2011	○ *Melt*, Tang Museum, Saratoga Springs, New York
	○ *Counterpart*, The West Collection, SEI Corporate Campus, Oaks, Pennsylvania.
	○ *Lady Gaga Could Shop Here*, Michael Rosenthal Gallery, San Francisco, California.
	○ *Williamsburg 2000*, Art 101, Brooklyn, New York.
	○ *Thinking Through Drawing*, The Macy Gallery, Teachers College, Columbia University, New York.
	○ *Subjective/Objective*, Pierogi, Brooklyn, New York.
2010	○ *Zeichnungen*, Graphiken und Fotografien aus New York und Leipzig, Kunstmühle, Mürsbach, Germany.
	○ *Mutant Anxiety*, Michael Rosenthal Gallery, San Francisco. California.
2009	○ *Eye World*, Triple Candie, New York, New York. (catalog)
	○ *Cream no Sugar*, Pierogi/Brooklyn, Brooklyn, New York.
	○ *Annual Biennial*, Michael Rosenthal Gallery, San Francisco, California.
	○ *Content/Discontent*; Friederike Taylor, New York, New York.
2008	○ *Pierogi, et. al.*, Daniel Weinberg Gallery, Los Angeles, California.
	○ *Art on Paper*, Weatherspoon Art Museum, Winston-Salem, North Carolina. (catalog)
	○ *Future Tense*, Neuberger Museum of Art, Purchase, New York. (video catalog)
2007	○ *Ho Hum All Ye Faithful*, Bravin Lee Programs, New York, New York.
2006	○ *Subverting the Status quo*, Axis Gallery, Sacramento, CA.
	○ *100 Artists, 100 Watercolors*, Jeannie Freilich Fine Art, New York, New York.
2005	○ *New Turf*, curated by Evelyn Hankins, Fleming Museum, University of Vermont, Burlington, Vermont. (catalog)
	○ *Pie Fight*, AR/Contemporary Gallery, Milan, Italy
	○ *Opening Bloom*, Barbara Davis Gallery, Houston, Texas
	○ *Faculty Show*, Usdan Gallery, Bennington College, Bennington, Vermont
	○ *American Obsessive Drawing*, Völcker and Freunde, Berlin, Germany. (catalog)

2004	○ *Open House*, The Brooklyn Museum of Art, Brooklyn, New York. (catalog)
	○ *Vacation Nation*, Pierogi, Brooklyn, New York.
2003	○ *BAM Next Next Wave Art*, curated by Dan Cameron, Brooklyn Academy of Music, NY.
	○ *In Heat*, Pierogi, Brooklyn, New York.
	○ *My Mother's An Artist*, curated by Sheila Pepe, Educational Alliance Gallery, New York.
	○ *Works on Paper*, Völcker & Freunde, Berlin, Germany.
	○ *Paintings, Drawings, Sculptures*, Greener Pastures Contemporary Art, Toronto, Ontario.
2002	○ *Hungry Eyes*, Dalhousie Art Gallery, Halifax, Nova Scotia.
	○ *Blobs, wiggles and dots*, curated by Lucio Pozzi, The Work Space, New York.
	○ *The Brooklyn Rail*, Selection I, curated by Phong Bui, Wythe Studio, Brooklyn, N.Y 25th Anniversary Benefit *Selections Exhibition*, The Drawing Center, New York, N.Y.
	○ *Touchy Feely*, Eyewash @ The Front Room, Brooklyn, New York.
	○ *Inter-sex-tion*, DNA Gallery, Provincetown, Massachusetts.
	○ *Need to Know Basis*, Geoffrey Young Gallery, Great Barrington, Massachusetts.

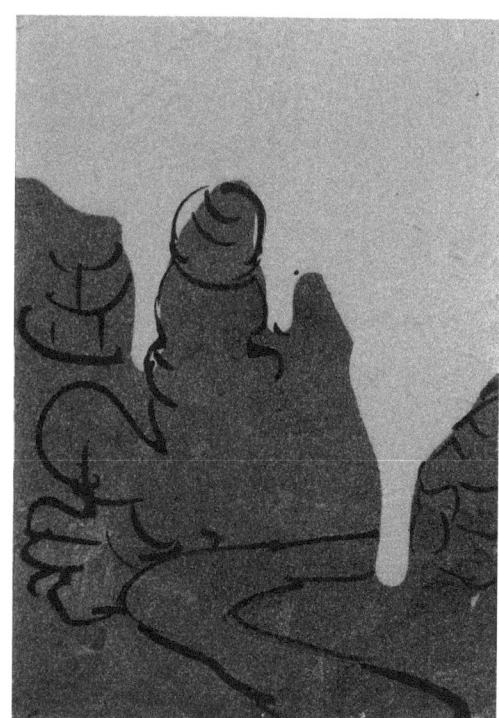

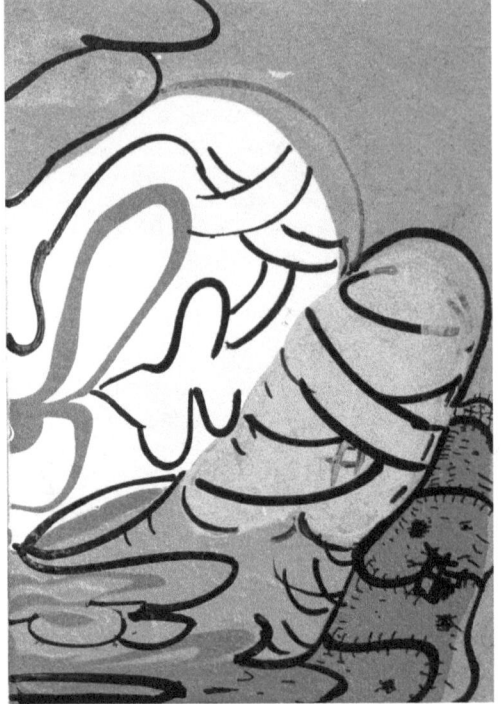

SELECTED GROUP EXHIBITIONS, CONTINUED

2001
- ◦ *Pop Science* (3-person show), g-module, Paris, France
- ◦ *New Prints*, Fall 2001, International Print Center, New York, New York
- ◦ *Compelled*, Hunterdon Art Museum, Clinton, New Jersey. (catalog)
- ◦ *Out of Hibernation*, Im in II, Brooklyn, New York.
- ◦ *Small Works*, Cape Museum of Fine Arts, Dennis, Massachusetts.

2000
- ◦ *Haulin' Ass*, Post Gallery, Los Angeles, California.
- ◦ *Superduper New York*, Pierogi 2000, Brooklyn, N.Y.
- ◦ *Art on Paper*, Weatherspoon Art Gallery, University of North Carolina at Greensboro.
- ◦ *@* , P.P.O.W., New York, N.Y.
- ◦ *Multiple Sensations*, Yerba Buena Center, San Francisco, California
- ◦ *Selections*, Eyewash, Brooklyn, N.Y.
- ◦ *Drawing*, Usdan Gallery, Bennington College, Bennington, Vermont.
- ◦ *Yaddo Centennia*; Art in General, N.Y., N.Y. and The Hyde Collection, Glens Falls, NY.

1999
- ◦ *Fields* (3-person show), P.P.O.W., New York, New York

- ◦ *Hard Cell*, Vilma Gold Gallery, London, England
- ◦ *Valentine*, Eyewash, Brooklyn, New York.
- ◦ *Range*, Chancellor's Gallery, State University, Albany, New York.

1998
- ◦ *Industrial Strength*, Warehouse, Exit Art, New York, N.Y.
- ◦ *Pierogi Goes to College*, Vassar College, Poughkeepsie, N.Y

1997
- ◦ *Current Undercurrent*, The Brooklyn Museum, Brooklyn, N.Y.
- ◦ *Redefinitions: A View from Brooklyn*, Fullerton Museum, California State University, Fullerton, California.
- ◦ *"...Just What Do You Think You're Doing Dave?"*, Williamsburg Art and Historical Center, Brooklyn, N.Y.

1996
- ◦ *Unconditionally Abstraction*, Schmidt Contemporary Art, St. Louis, Missouri.
- ◦ *Central Industrial Supply Show*, Central Industrial Supply, New York, N.Y.

1995
- ◦ *Jane Fine, Joanne Greenbaum, John-Paul Philippe*, Arena, Brooklyn, N.Y.
- ◦ *Wacko*, The Work Space, New York, N.Y.
- ◦ *Works for a Funhouse*, E.S.Vandam, New York, N.Y.
- ◦ *Other Rooms*, Ronald Feldman Fine Art, New York, N.Y.

1994
- ◦ *Paintings*, Friedrich Petzel Gallery, New York, N.Y.
- ◦ *The New Pop*, Leo Tony Gallery, New York, N.Y.
- ◦ *Spirit of New York*, Spazio Emilo de Marchi, Milan, Italy
- ◦ *Crest Hardware Show*, Brooklyn, N.Y.
- ◦ *Animated*, Art in General, New York, N.Y.

1993
- ◦ *Pure Pop for Now People*, Jack Tilton Gallery, New York, N.Y.

1992
- ◦ *Update 1992*, White Columns, New York, N.Y.
- ◦ *Salon of the Mating Spiders*, Herron Test Site, Brooklyn, N.Y.

1991
- ◦ *High Density Abstraction*, Procter Art Center, Bard College, Annandale-on Hudson, N.Y.

1988
- ◦ *Selections 42*, The Drawing Center, New York, N.Y.

SELECTED BIBLIOGRAPHY

- ◦ D. Eric Bookhardt, *Review: Works by Chris Guarisco, James Esber and Jane Fine*, Best of New Orleans.com, March 19, 2013.
- ◦ Eric Gelber, *Jane Fine in Melt at The Tang*, artcritical.com, July 24, 2011
- ◦ Kenneth Baker, *Fine Shines at Rosenthal*, **San Francisco Chronicle**, April 3, 2010.
- ◦ Will Corwin, *Jane Fine*, **Art Papers**, January/February 2010, Vol. 34, No. 1, p. 64.
- ◦ Stephen Maine, *Jane Fine/Pierogi*, **Art in America**, December 2009, Vol. 97, No. 11, p. 140.
- ◦ Patrick Knowles, "Mutant Anxiety": Angst, Woes in Colorful Veins, **San Francisco Chronicle**, December 31, 2009.
- ◦ Jim Supanick, *"Makin' Whopee: A Conversation with J. Fiber; James Esber and Jane Fine,"* **The Brooklyn Rail**, April 2008, pp. 29 – 33.

○ Iris Marble Cushing, *"J. Fiber in Brooklyn,"* **ArtInfo.com**, published March 27, 2008.
○ Owen Roberts, *"J. Fiber and Yoon Lee at Williamsburg's Pierogi,"* (gowanuslounge.blogspot.com), p March 20, 2008.
○ *Jane Fine*: **Border Patrol**, USB Magazine, February 2008, p. 48.
○ Pamela Polston, *Finding her Place*, **Seven Days**, July 13, 2005.
○ Benjamin Genocchio, *What is War Good For? Art*, **The New York Times**, January 9, 2005.
○ Gregory Volk, *Big Brash Borough*, **Art in America**, September 2004, No. 8, pp. 93-97 and 142.
○ Holland Cotter, *Brooklyn-ness, a State of Mind and Artistic Identity in the un-Chelsea*, **The New York Times**, April 16, 2004
○ *Galleries: Brooklyn - Jane Fine/Reed Anderson*, **The New Yorker**, April 19 & 26, 2004.
○ Ken Johnson, *Art in Review: Jane Fine: After Sugar Time*, **The New York Times**, April 2, 2004.
○ Stephen Maine, Dateline Brooklyn, **artnet.com**, April 2004.
○ *My Mother's An Artist*, **The New Yorker,** May 26, 2003.
○ Sarah Hartland-Rowe, *Around and About Painting*, **Border Crossings**, Volume 22, No. 1, Issue 85.
○ Sarah Hollenberg, *Hungry Eyes*, **The Brooklyn Rail**, Winter 2003.
○ Alice Burdick, *Hungry Eyes*, **Arts Atlantic**, Spring 2003, No. 74.

○ Monica Tap, *Hungry Eyes* (catalog essay), **Dalhousie Art Gallery**, Nova Scotia, 2002.
○ Holland Cotter, *Last Chance: The Brooklyn Rail: Selection 1*, **The New York Times**, March 1, 2002.
○ Faye Hirsch, *Working Proof: Jane Fine*, **Art on Paper**, Volume 6, Number 4, March - April, 2002.
○ Dan Bischoff, *The Labor Defines the Art in Hunterdon*, **Newark Star Ledger**, September 30, 2001.
○ Audrey Techer, *Americans in Paris*, **Post: Review of Contemporary Art**, No. 5, February 2001.
○ Holland Cotter, *For Hikers Seeking Art Brooklyn is a Left Bank*, **The New York Times**, Dec. 15, 2000.
○ *Galleries - Brooklyn: Jane Fine*, **The New Yorker**, November 27, 2000.
○ James Kalm, *Jane Fine @ Pierogi*, **NY Arts**, Volume 6, Number 1, January 20001.
○ Giovanni Garcia-Fenech, *Brooklyn Spice*, **Artnet.com/Magazine**, January 5, 2001.
○ Carol Vogel, *Inside Art*, **The New York Times**, June 9, 2000.
○ Rachel Youens, *The Local Scene*, **The Brooklyn Rail**, Issue 43/44, December/January 2000/2001.
○ Cathy Curtis, *A Bridge to Brooklyn*, **The Los Angeles Time**s, November 18, 1997.
○ Daniella Walsh, *Brooklyn Art Pays a Visit to Fullerton*, **The Orange Country Register**, November 23, 1997.
○ Roberta Smith, *Palettes Full of Ideas About What Painting Should Be*, **The New York Times**, November 1, 1996.
○ Roberta Smith, *Art in Review: Jane Fine*, **The New York Times**, April 14, 1995.
○ Stuart Servetar, *Jane Fine*, **New York Press**, April 12, 1995.
○ Stuart Servetar, *The New Pop*, **New York Press**, July 6, 1994.
○ *In volo "spiriti" newyorkesi*, **Lombardia Oggi**, June 26, 1994.
○ Marina Mojana, *Scoprendo l'America a Milano*, **Il Sole 24 Ore**, June 19, 1994.
○ Stuart Servetar, *Animated*, **New York Press**, June 1, 1994.
○ Roberta Smith, *Shades of a Rebirth for Painting*, **The New York Times**, June 18, 1993.
○ *Lo Spirito di New York*, **L'Informazione**, June 14, 1994.
○ Kim Levin, *Choices*, **Village Voice**, June 23, 1993

PUBLIC COLLECTIONS

○ The Tang Teaching Museum at Skidmore College
○ The Neuberger Museum of Art
○ Fogg Art Museum/Harvard University Museums
○ The West Collection
○ The Aspen Collection
○ The Chaney Family Collection
○ Progressive Corporation
○ Fidelity Investments
○ The Graham Gund Collection
○ Saks Fifth Avenue Collection

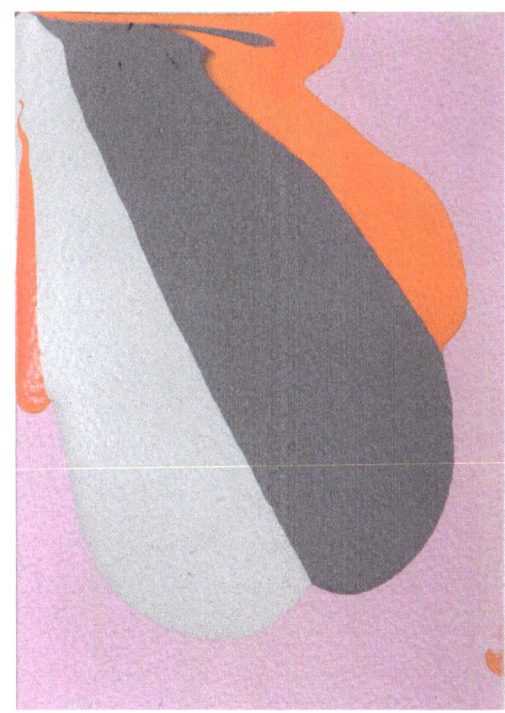

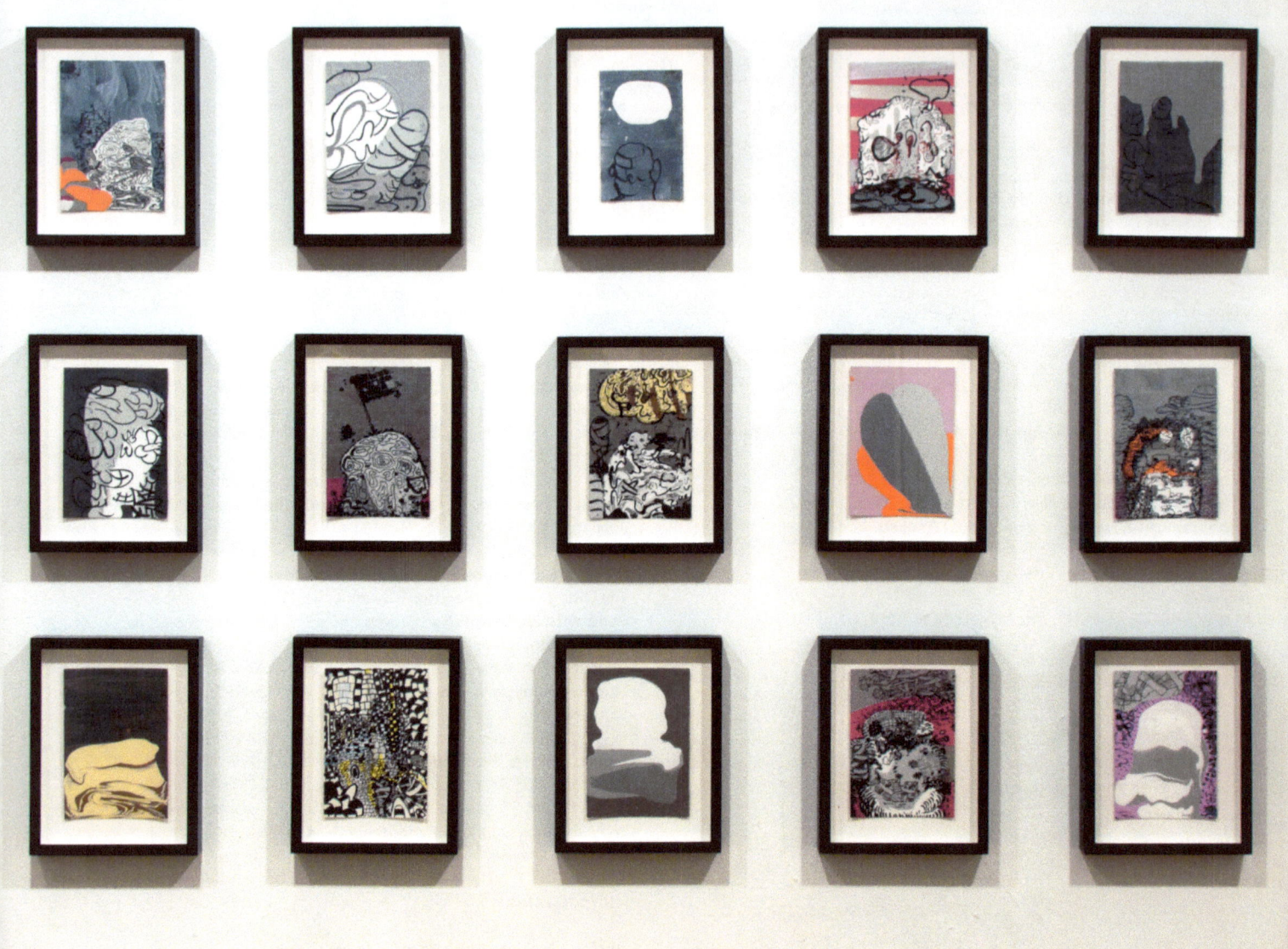

EMERGENCY ALERT SYSTEM

[SUITE OF 15 PAINTINGS]
2015, acrylic and ink on paper, 6" x 4 " - 7" x 5".
Installation view. *Pages 11; 36-39*: selected paintings
from installation.

www.ingramcontent.com/pod-product-compliance
Lightning Source LLC
Chambersburg PA
CBHW050840180526
45159CB00004B/1974